Excel Construction Kit #1
Year Planner Application

In this book you will learn how to use and apply advanced Excel ski
business application:

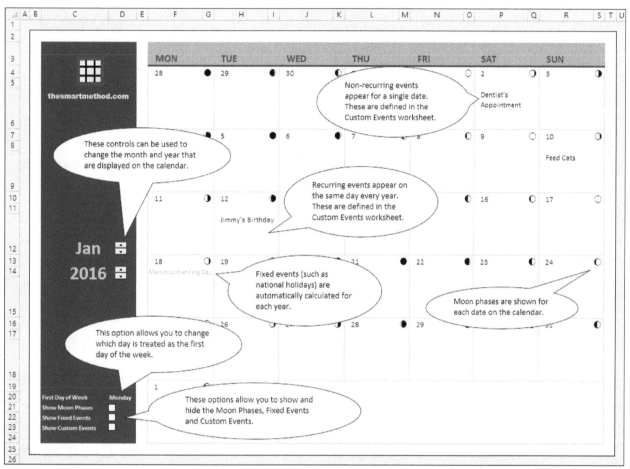

Users can define both recurring and non-recurring events:

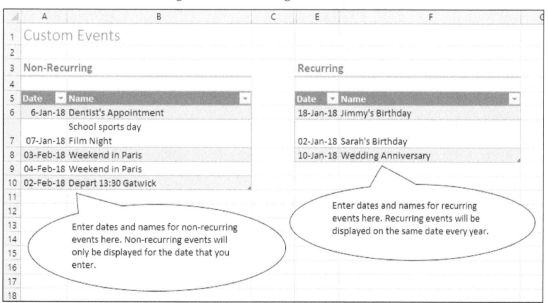

Learning by doing.
An alternative approach to learning and applying Excel skills

For over 900 years craftsmen have traditionally taught their skills to an apprentice. The apprentice would work (often unpaid) for a period of five to nine years to learn the craftsman's trade. In this model the apprentice learned his trade by observing how the master craftsman used his skills. The apprentice would then attempt to imitate the same techniques.

This construction kit will teach you advanced Excel skills in the same way. Even if you only have basic Excel skills, the construction kit is designed in such a way that you'll be able to construct a complex, polished professional Excel application that would be well beyond the powers of most advanced Excel users.

As you progress through the book you will use advanced Excel skills to construct a finished application. Along the way you'll learn Excel techniques that you will be able to apply in the future to a multitude of Excel business problems.

No VBA program code or Macros are used in this construction project.

 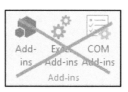

The use of VBA programming code or recorded macros (recorded macros also contain VBA program code) is always a virus threat. For this reason, most corporate environments have a security policy that does not allow VBA program code within Excel workbooks.

When using Excel for its intended purpose it is actually very rare find a true need for custom VBA program code.

No VBA program code, recorded macros or add-ins are used in the sophisticated project you'll build using this book. You will complete your construction kit using only regular Excel features.

This book will teach you best-practice when applying your Excel skills to large real-world projects.

This book won't only teach you Excel skills. You'll also learn a best-practice design and development methodology that will stand you in good stead when working on future Excel projects.

In constructing this project you'll discover new and interesting ways to use many of Excel 2019's more powerful and complex features.

Use of this book as courseware

This book is particularly useful for training organizations, teachers, schools, colleges and universities who would like to engage, motivate and interest students by having them use Excel skills to produce an interesting, useful and impressive Excel application.

You can use this construction kit in two ways

As an Excel beginner

If you are an absolute beginner who has never used Excel before you'll need to acquire some basic skills before beginning this construction kit. We offer a free *Excel Basic Skills* tutorial on our thesmartmethod.com website as a free e-book and on-line video. This covers the bare minimum skills you'll need to get started.

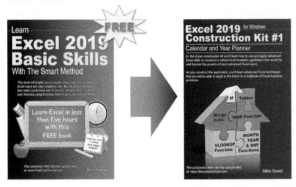

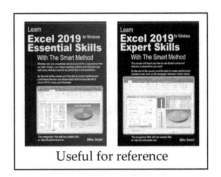

Useful for reference

If you follow this track, you'll still learn a lot of useful information (and hopefully have fun along the way), but you'll only have a surface-level understanding of some of the Expert-level skills you'll use. You'll also have a more limited knowledge of Excel as you'll only discover the features that you use in the construction kit.

It isn't necessary to have the *Essential Skills* and *Expert Skills* books (or e-books) on hand to complete this construction kit but it is highly recommended that you do.

The *Essential Skills* and *Expert Skills* tutorials provide an in-depth understanding of all the advanced features used in this construction kit. If you have the books (or e-books) on hand, you'll be able to use them as a reference to expand your understanding of some of the advanced skills you will use in this construction kit.

As an Excel Expert

If you've already completed our *Essential Skills* and *Expert Skills* tutorials you already have advanced Excel skills that are rarely mastered by the average user.

This construction kit will show expert users how to plan and implement a high-quality Excel solution. You'll learn a solid design methodology that will enable you to use and apply your skills to satisfy even the most complex business requirements.

You will also discover some innovative techniques that combine Excel's advanced features to elegantly solve complex requirements.

Every step in your construction kit is presented on two facing pages

Pray this day, on one side of one sheet of paper, explain how the Royal Navy is prepared to meet the coming conflict.
Winston Churchill, Letter to the Admiralty, Sep 1, 1939

Winston Churchill was well aware of the power of brevity. The discipline of condensing thoughts into one side of a single sheet of A4 paper resulted in the efficient transfer of information.

A tenet of our teaching system is that every step in this construction kit is presented on *two* facing sheets of A4. We've had to double Churchill's rule as they didn't have to contend with screen grabs in 1939! If we can't teach an essential concept in two pages of A4 we know that the subject matter needs to be broken into two smaller lessons.

How this book avoids wasting your time.

Many presentational methods have been used in this book to help you to skip reading about things you already know how to do, or things that are of little interest to you.

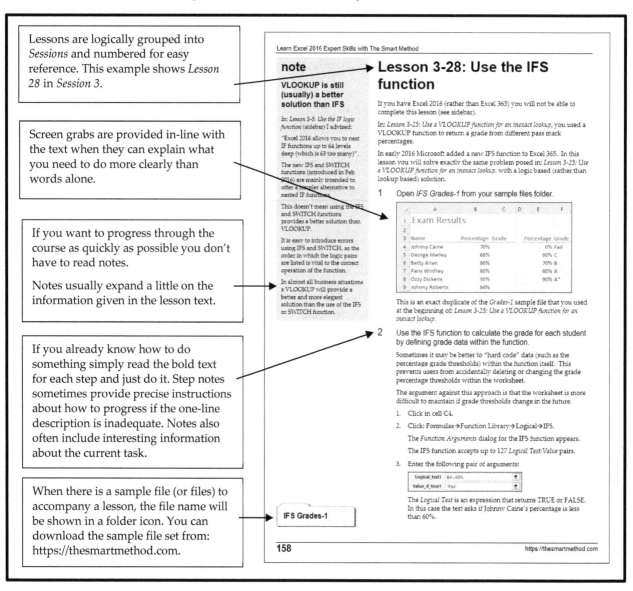

Learning by participation

> Tell me, and I will forget. Show me, and I may remember. Involve me, and I will understand.
>
> *Confucius, Chinese teacher, editor, politician and philosopher (551-479 BC)*

Confucius would probably have agreed that the best way to teach IT skills is hands-on (actively) and not hands-off (passively). This is another of the principal tenets of The Smart Method® teaching method.

Research has backed up the assertion that you will learn more material, learn more quickly, and understand more of what you learn if you learn using active, rather than passive methods.

For this reason, pure theory pages are kept to an absolute minimum with most theory woven into the hands-on lessons, either within the text or in sidebars.

This echoes the teaching method used in Smart Method classroom courses where snippets of pertinent theory are woven into the lessons themselves so that interest and attention is maintained by hands-on involvement, but all necessary theory is still covered.

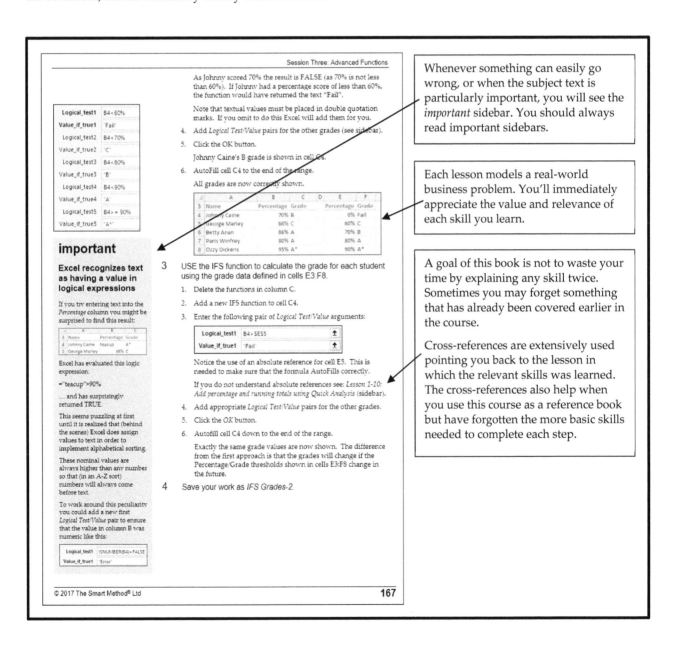

What you will learn

In the process of completing this construction kit, you'll learn how to apply many Excel skills in the context of a real-world project.

Here are some of the skills you will use (in the order that they first appear in the book).

- Understand the Waterfall Method.
- Understand update channels and enable automatic updates.
- Apply background colors.
- Specify a custom color using RGB values.
- Create a Custom Color Set.
- Enable and disable gridlines.
- Apply Borders and Lines.
- Select non-contiguous cells, rows and columns.
- Resize rows and columns.
- Use AutoFill.
- Set vertical and horizontal cell alignment.
- Set cell indents.
- Set font sizes and colors.
- Wrap text.
- Merge cells.
- Use custom formats.
- Create line breaks within custom formats.
- Insert Symbols into cells.
- Insert pictures into a worksheet.
- Use a Spin Button Form Control.
- Use a Checkbox Form Control.
- Insert and name worksheets.
- Create a Tables.
- Name a Table.
- Apply Cell Styles.
- Work with shapes.
- Define named ranges and named cells.
- Use the Name Manager to view, delete and edit range names.
- Create a drop-down list using a list validation.
- Understand and use control settings.
- Understand and use helper cells.

- AutoSize columns.

- Use the IF logical function.

- Understand Date Serial Numbers.

- Use the DATE function.

- Understand international date formats (MDY and DMY).

- Use the WEEKDAY function.

- Understand precedence rules.

- Format date serial numbers using a custom format.

- Use the TEXT function.

- Use the UPPER function.

- Use a cell link to connect a Spin Button control to a control setting.

- Understand magic numbers.

- Create a formula driven conditional format.

- Use the MONTH function.

- Use the Conditional Format Rules Manager.

- Use the OR logical function.

- Understand the AND, NOT and XOR logical functions.

- Use absolute, relative and mixed cell references.

- Calculate the correct date for New Year's Day (in any year) using the DATE function.

- Link a table of fixed events to the calendar so that fixed events are appropriately displayed.

- Use the VLOOKUP function.

- Use the IFERROR function.

- AutoFill formulas.

- Copy and Paste.

- Understand calculated table columns.

- Calculate the correct dates for New Year's Day, Independence Day, Christmas Day and Veterans' Day (for any year) using the DATE function.

- Calculate the correct date for Martin Luther King Day, President's Day, Labor Day, Columbus Day and Thanksgiving Day (in any year) using simple Excel formulas and helper cells.

- Understand the CHOOSE function.

- Calculate the correct date for Memorial Day (in any year) using simple Excel formulas and helper cells.

- Understand symbolic constants and how they can be used to give meaning to magic numbers.

- Calculate the correct date for Easter Sunday (in any year).

- Add a unique constraint to a table using a formula-driven data validation.

- Understand the COUNTIF and COUNTIFS functions.

- Use structured table references.

- Use the CHAR function.

- Understand the CODE function.

- Concatenate text.

- Create a text length data validation.

- Calculate the age of the moon using Synodic Months and the MOD function.

- Calculate the correct phase of the moon (for any date) based upon the moon's age.

- Use the ROW function.

- Use Excel's zoom feature.

- Use Paste Formulas to copy formulas without disturbing conditional formatting.

- Create user-friendly validation error messages.

- Hide error warning markers.

- Use Smart Tags.

- Unlock cells.

- Hide columns and entire worksheets.

- Protect a worksheet to prevent users from making unwanted changes.

Excel 2019 Construction Kit #1

Calendar and Year Planner

Mike Smart

Excel 2019 Construction Kit #1: Calendar and Year Planner

Published by:

The Smart Method® Ltd
Burleigh Manor
Peel Road
Douglas, IOM
Great Britain
IM1 5EP

Tel: +44 (0)845 458 3282 Fax: +44 (0)845 458 3281

E-mail: Use the contact page at https://TheSmartMethod.com/contact
Web: https://TheSmartMethod.com (this book's dedicated web site)

International Standard Book Number (ISBN13): 978-1-909253-36-0

The Smart Method® is a registered trademark of The Smart Method Ltd.

2 4 6 8 10 9 7 5 3 1

Contents

Introduction

Welcome to *Excel 2019 Construction Kit #1: Calendar and Year Planner*. This book has been designed to enable students to apply their existing advanced Excel skills to the construction of a polished and professional Excel application. The book is equally useful as courseware to deliver classroom courses.

Smart Method® publications are continually evolving as we discover better ways of explaining or teaching the concepts presented.

Feedback

At The Smart Method® we love feedback – both positive and negative. If you have any suggestions for improvements to future versions of this book, or if you find content or typographical errors, the author would always love to hear from you.

You can make suggestions for improvements to this book using the online form at:

https://thesmartmethod.com/contact/

Future editions of this book will always incorporate your feedback so that there are never any known errors at time of publication.

If you have any difficulty understanding or completing a lesson, or if you feel that anything could have been more clearly explained, we'd also love to hear from you. We've made hundreds of detail improvements to our books based upon reader's feedback and continue to chase the impossible goal of 100% perfection.

Downloading the sample files

In order to use this book, it is necessary to download sample files from the Internet. The sample files are available from:

http://thesmartmethod.com

Type the above URL into your web browser and you'll see the link to the sample files at the top of the home page.

Problem resolution

If you encounter any problem using any aspect of the course you can contact us using the online form at:

https://thesmartmethod.com/contact/

We'll do everything possible to quickly resolve the problem.

The Excel versions that were used to write this book

This edition was written using both the *Excel 2019* perpetual license (the one-time payment version) and *Excel 365* (semi-annual version 1808, released on Jan 01 2019). You'll discover which version your computer is running in: *Lesson 2-1: Check that your Excel version is up to date.*

This book is written purely for Excel 2019 and Excel 365, though readers may find some of the content is also applicable to earlier Excel versions.

Typographical Conventions Used in This Book

This guide consistently uses typographical conventions to differentiate parts of the text.

When you see this	Here's what it means
Click *Line Color* on the left-hand bar and then click *No line.*	Italics are used to refer to text that appears in a worksheet cell, an Excel dialog, on the Ribbon, or elsewhere within the Excel application. Italics may sometimes also be used for emphasis or distinction.
Click: Home→Font→Underline. 	Click on the Ribbon's *Home* tab and then look for the *Font* group. Click the *Underline* button within this group (that's the left-hand side of the button, not the drop-down arrow next to it). Don't worry if this doesn't make sense yet. We cover the Ribbon in depth in session one.
Click: Home→Font→ Underline Drop Down→Double Underline. 	Click on the Ribbon's *Home* tab and then look for the *Font* group. Click the drop-down arrow next to the Underline button (that's the right-hand side of the button) within this group and then choose *Double Underline* from the drop-down list.
Click: File→Options→ Advanced→General→ Edit Custom Lists→Import	This is a more involved example. 1. Click the *File* tab on the Ribbon, and then click the *Options* button towards the bottom of the left-hand pane. The *Excel Options* dialog appears. 2. Choose the *Advanced* list item in the left-hand pane and scroll down to the *General* group in the right-hand pane. 3. Click the *Edit Custom Lists…* button. Yet another dialog pops up. 4. Click the *Import* button.
Type: **European Sales** into the cell.	Whenever you are supposed to actually type something on the keyboard it is shown in bold faced text.
Press <Ctrl> + <Z>.	You should hold down the **Ctrl** key and then press the **Z** key.

| ∑ AutoSum ▾ | When a lesson tells you to click a button, an image of the relevant button will often be shown either in the page margin or within the text itself. |

note

An Excel worksheet can contain up to 16,585 columns and 1,048,476 rows.

If you want to read through the book as quickly as possible, you don't have to read notes.

Notes usually expand a little on the information given in the lesson text.

important

Do not click the *Delete* button at this point as to do so would erase the entire table.

Whenever something can easily go wrong, or when the subject text is particularly important, you will see the *important* sidebar.

You should always read important sidebars.

tip

Moving between tabs using the keyboard

You can also use the
<Ctrl>+<PgUp> and
<Ctrl>+<PgDn> keyboard
shortcuts to cycle through all of the tabs in your workbook.

Tips add to the lesson text by showing you shortcuts or time-saving techniques relevant to the lesson.

The bold text at the top of the tip box enables you to establish whether the tip is appropriate to your needs without reading all of the text.

In this example you may not be interested in keyboard shortcuts so do not need to read further.

anecdote

I ran an Excel course for a small company in London a couple of years ago...

Sometimes I add an anecdote gathered over the years from my Excel classes or from other areas of life.

If you simply want to learn Excel as quickly as possible you can ignore my anecdotes.

trivia

The feature that Excel uses to help you out with function calls first made an appearance in Visual Basic 5 back in 1996 ...

Sometimes I indulge myself by adding a little piece of trivia in the context of the skill being taught.

Just like my anecdotes you can ignore these if you want to. They won't help you to learn Excel any better!

| **The World's Fastest Cars** | When there is a sample file (or files) to accompany a lesson, the file name will be shown in a folder icon. You can download the sample file from: http://thesmartmethod.com. |

How to use this construction kit

Three important rules

#1 - Complete the construction kit from beginning to end

Just like a real-world construction project you need to start at the beginning and progress, one lesson at a time, until you have completed the application.

When you have finished your project, you can re-do specific lessons by using any of the incremental sample files to regress to any point in the construction process.

#2 If possible, complete a session in one sitting

The book is arranged into *sessions* and *lessons* (each presented upon two facing pages).

You can complete as many, or as few, lessons as you have the time and energy for each day. Many learners have completed their construction kit by setting aside just a few minutes each day to complete a single lesson.

If it is possible, the most effective way to learn is to lock yourself away, switch off your telephone, and complete a full session, without interruption, except for a 15-minute break each hour. The memory process is associative, and we've ensured that the lessons in each session are very closely coupled (contextually) with the others. By completing the whole session in one sitting, you'll store all that information in the same part of your memory and will find it easier to recall later.

The experience of being able to remember all the words of a song as soon as somebody has got you "started" with the first line is an example of the memory's associative system of data storage.

#3 Rest at least every hour

In our classroom courses we have often observed a phenomenon that we call "running into a wall". This happens when a student becomes overloaded with new information to the point that they can no longer follow the simplest instruction. If you find this happening to you, you've studied for too long without a rest.

You should take a 15-minute break every hour (or more often if you begin to feel overwhelmed) and spend it relaxing rather than catching up with your e-mails. Ideally you should relax by lying down and closing your eyes. This allows your brain to use all its processing power to efficiently store and index the skills you've learned. We've found that this hugely improves retention.

How to best use the incremental sample files

All lessons in this construction kit (apart from those that have no hands-on tasks) use a sample file that is incrementally improved during each lesson. At the end of each lesson an interim version is always saved. The first file you will save will be called *Year Planner-1*. You will then begin the following lesson with the *Year Planner-1* file and then save it (after completing all lesson steps) as *Year Planner-2*. By the end of the construction kit you'll be up to *Year Planner-43* (the finished application).

A complete set of sample files (including all incremental versions) are provided in the sample file set. This provides three important benefits:

- If you have difficulty with a lesson it is useful to be able to study the completed workbook (at the end of the lesson) by opening the finished version of the lesson's workbook.

- When you have completed the book, you may want to revise some of the steps that you used to complete it (perhaps to use the same skills in another project). The sample files allow you to work through any single lesson in isolation, as the workbook's state at the beginning of each lesson is always available.

- When teaching a class one student may corrupt their workbook by a series of errors (or by their computer crashing). It is possible to move the class on quickly and easily to the next lesson by instructing the student to open the next sample file in the set (instead of progressing with their own corrupted file or copying a file from another student).

Blank page

Session One: Methodology & Functional Specification

Imagine you are building a house. You wouldn't just race into a field and start digging foundations. You'd begin by employing an architect to carefully design every aspect of the finished house.

You wouldn't begin building the house until everything had been carefully designed and documented. In other words, you'd have to know exactly what you were building before you started building it.

You'd be amazed to know that in the world of business, most real-world software projects are not planned quite so well. In fact, some are not designed and documented at all. It is often the case that managers don't understand the need for a design phase and expect developers to begin construction on the first day of a project.

Methodology

This construction kit uses a high-quality application development methodology sometimes called the waterfall model. If you use this approach, you'll develop higher quality solutions faster – no matter how small the project is.

The basis of the waterfall model was first defined in 1970 by a paper authored by Winston W. Royce (a computer scientist at Lockheed working on the space program).

Winston had spent nine years developing software for spacecraft mission planning, commanding and post-flight analysis. His 1970 paper distilled his vast experience into the observation that software development consisted of two steps: Analysis and Coding. More simply put, you have to figure out what you need to do before you actually do it.

Winston observed, however, that in larger systems, any project that included *only* these two steps was "doomed to failure". In this session you'll learn how to use Winston's waterfall model. Even though this is a simple application, you'll still use the waterfall model to design it.

The Functional Specification

The waterfall model requires that every project should begin with a *Functional Specification.*

It may seem like overkill to have a functional specification for such a small project, but as you progress through the construction kit you'll appreciate the usefulness of this approach. You'll also realize how much longer everything would have taken if you hadn't specified what you needed to do before starting.

Lesson 1-1: Understand the Waterfall Model

How the waterfall methodology is used in this construction kit

During my own career developing large software systems (for corporate clients in different business areas) I have discovered many different names given to the steps originally identified by Winston Royce. Here are my preferred names for the steps you need to successfully complete a project along, with their many aliases:

Step One: Functional Specification

Other names: Requirements Specification, Requirements Analysis, Requirements Definition, Software Requirements, Specification, Spec, Analysis, Project Analysis Document, Problem Statement, Conceptual Design, Goal Centered Design, Logical Design.

What it really means: What the application needs to do, but not what it will look like or how it will do it.

Your users will need to sign-off on the *Functional Specification* before you proceed to the *User Interface*.

Step Two: User Interface

Other names: Prototype, User Interface Design, User Interface Specification.

What it really means: What the application looks like and how it will deliver the requirements detailed in the *Functional Specification*.

Later, in: *Session Two: Create the User Interface,* you'll design a user interface that will show how all of the features described in the functional specification will be delivered.

You'll deliver the user interface as a non-functioning, annotated Excel workbook. This can then be shared amongst your users to make sure they are happy with the final appearance and how the application will work before you spend time making everything work.

Step Three: Construction

Other names: Coding, Implementation, Coding & Debugging, Programming.

What it really means: Making everything in the user interface work as specified.

In the construction phase you'll go on to make the features that were specified in the *functional specification* work using the *user interface* you have designed.

Step Four: Testing

Other names: System Testing, Integration Testing, Acceptance Testing.

What it really means: Working through the Functional Specification and making sure that the finished application reliably and correctly provides all of the functionality that was specified there.

How the four phases of the waterfall model work together

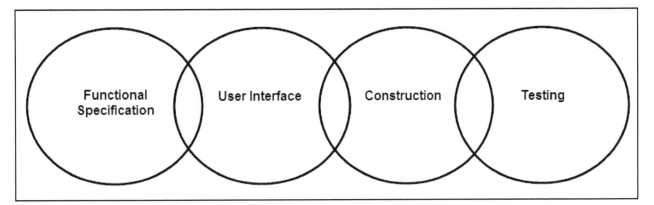

note

In 1985 the United States government published a document titled: *Defense Systems Software Development (DOD-STD-2167A).*

This document broadly describes the Waterfall Method as the preferred standard for software development.

The document defined six phases (an elaboration of the four described in this lesson):

- Preliminary Design
- Detailed Design
- Coding
- Unit Testing
- Integration
- Testing

You'll learn more about unit testing and integration testing in: *Lesson 7-4: Remove test data and finalize the year planner.*

The above diagram shows how the *Functional Specification* and *User Interface* fit into the overall development process. You can see that each process overlaps. This is designed to indicate some degree of interaction between each step and the preceding step. In other words, users may see the *User Interface* and then realize that it doesn't cater for a requirement that should properly have been included in the *Functional Specification*. At this stage, the uncaptured requirement can be added to the *Functional Specification* and incorporated into the *User Interface*.

You should only ever re-iterate to the previous step

The waterfall model insists that there should be no overlap other than with the preceding step.

This means that once the functional specification and user interface have been agreed, development can only proceed efficiently if no further functionality is added to the current version.

Any late requests for enhancements should form the subject of a new functional specification for the second release and you should not try to incorporate them into the current version. This is an **absolutely essential** discipline for efficient software development.

You can see now why Winston's methodology has been called the *waterfall model*. Water only flows one way in a waterfall, just as the project flows from left to right in the diagram above (but never from right to left).

Lesson 1-2: Understand the structure of a functional specification

A good functional specification completely describes an application without considering what the user interface will look like or how the functionality will be implemented.

The functional specification should describe all of the things that the application needs to do.

Make sure that the functional specification describes what the application does and not how it will do it

I've organized many meetings with business experts to draw up a functional specification for a new software solution. Some have been for very large systems with functional specifications stretching to over 200 pages.

At the beginning of the meeting I always emphasize that users are not allowed to talk about the user interface when describing functionality. Of course, they always do, and I have to work hard to steer them back to functionality.

For example, a user will say something like:

"We need a drop-down list showing different countries and when you click on a country a box will pop up showing year-to-date sales for the current year".

The user needs to be brought back onto track to state the actual requirement as:

"It must be possible to quickly view year-to-date sales for any country".

Later, when the user interface is designed, the users can see how it is proposed to deliver the functionality defined in the functional specification. This may be very different from the way in which the user originally visualized it.

Staying focused in this way will allow you to capture the requirements of the business far more precisely.

The three main sections of a functional specification

Mission statement

"There are no big problems, there are just a lot of little problems."

Henry Ford, founder of the Ford Motor Company (1863-1947)

Important

Always organize a sign-off meeting for the functional specification

I have discovered that if you simply e-mail a functional specification to a client for review it is rare for anybody to invest the time needed to read it.

The functional specification is hugely important as it defines success. Your project will demonstrably be a success if it delivers all the functionality defined in the functional specification.

If you don't make sure that the functional specification is accurate you are setting yourself up for failure when you deliver the finished application.

I have found it best to organize a meeting of stakeholders including business experts and the actual end-users of the application.

Read out each requirement at the meeting and invite questions. You'd be amazed how many new requirements you will capture by doing this.

I've often had to organize a second meeting to review version 2 of the functional specification as it had to be completely re-written after the first sign-off meeting.

The best way to start a functional specification is with a mission statement. You need to turn Henry Ford's words upside down and appreciate that the project will solve lots of little problems but can also be described in a more abstract way as one big problem.

Ideally your mission statement will consist of a single sentence, but it could also be extended to two or three sentences.

You'll see the mission statement for this construction kit later, in: *Lesson 1-3: The Functional Specification.*

Primary business objectives

Having defined the mission statement, the primary business objectives now flesh out the requirement in a little more detail.

There will normally be less than ten primary business objectives even in a large system.

You'll see the primary business objectives for this construction kit later, in: *Lesson 1-3: The Functional Specification.*

Requirements

Having defined the *mission statement* and the *primary business objectives*, the requirements now express in detail the precise functionality that the system needs to deliver.

You'll see the requirements for this construction kit later, in: *Lesson 1-3: The Functional Specification.*

Lesson 1-3: The Functional Specification

Here is the functional specification for the application you are about to create.

When the application is complete it will be possible to test it against this functional specification to confirm that all of the features specified have been delivered.

Mission Statement

To create a year planner that can be easily be populated with different date-related events.

Primary Business Objectives

1. Provide a calendar that will show an entire month of dates and events.

2. Allow the user to quickly select any year or month.

3. Allow the user to select Sunday or Monday as the first day of the week.

4. Show the phase of the moon for each date.

5. Allow one fixed event (such as Christmas Day or New Year's Day) to be displayed for each date.

6. Display custom events defined by the user for each date (such as appointments or birthdays).

7. Allow both fixed and custom events to recur each year if required.

8. Allow users to customize the calendar by enabling or disabling event types that they may have no use for.

9. Ensure that the finished calendar looks professional when printed.

Requirements

1. **Supported date range**

    The calendar needs to support, as a minimum, all dates up to 100 years in the past and up to 100 years in the future. For the purposes of this specification this will mean the date range: 1st January 1918 to 1st January 2118.

2. **Information to be shown for each date**

    2.1. The calendar will always show 37 days, starting with the Monday or Sunday on or before the 1st of the month that is being displayed.

    2.2. Moon Phase

    For every date in the supported date range, it should be clearly indicated which phase of the moon is active. Eight different phases of the moon should be displayed:

    - New Moon

    - Waxing Crescent

    - First Quarter

    - Waxing Gibbous

    - Full Moon

- Waning Gibbous
- Last Quarter
- Waning Crescent

3. Fixed events

The following fixed events will be automatically calculated and included (for every year):

- New Year's Day
- Martin Luther King Day
- Presidents' Day
- Easter Sunday
- Memorial Day
- Independence Day
- Labor Day
- Columbus Day
- Veteran's Day
- Thanksgiving Day
- Christmas Day

4. Custom events

4.1. It must be possible for a user to quickly define several custom events for each day (such as a birthday, holiday or appointment).

4.2. Events must be restricted to the visible space available for display for each calendar day without scrolling.

4.3. It must be possible to define custom events that are up to 32 characters (in total) long for each day.

5. Recurring events

It must be possible for a user to define each custom event as recurring or non-recurring. A recurring event is defined as an event that will occur on the same date of every year in the supported date range.

6. Calendar Settings

6.1. Customization of calendar display

It must be possible to show or hide Moon Phases, Fixed Events and Custom Events.

6.2. First day of the week

It must be possible to define either Sunday or Monday as the first day of the week.

7. Usability

7.1. The user must not need any Excel skills or training

7.2. The year planner must be intuitive and easy to use for untrained users.

7.3. On-screen help must be provided whenever the purpose of any on-screen item is not obvious.

8. Compact design

8.1. The main features of the application should be designed so that users do not have to scroll their screens when using a standard 22-inch monitor (providing a resolution of 1680X1050).

8.2. The calendar should appear professional and legible when printed upon one sheet of Letter-Sized or A4 paper (in landscape orientation).

9. Security

9.1. It must not be possible for a user to break any of the functionality of the application in normal use.

9.2. The implementation must not make use of any VBA or macro code.

Session Two: Create the User Interface

Good looks only take you so far.

Angie Everhart, American Actress (1969-)

When the functional specification has been completed and (most importantly) signed off by users, the next step will be to design the user interface.

In this lesson you'll design the visual appearance of the year planner application. You can then submit the workbook to users for approval before you move on to make each feature work.

Sometimes users will see the user interface and then identify new requirements that were missed when the functional specification was agreed.

In: *Lesson 1-1: Understand the Waterfall Model*, you learned that it is permissible to re-visit the functional specification if new requirements are identified as a result of making a non-functioning user interface available to users.

Session Objectives

By the end of this session you will have:

- Checked that your Excel version is up to date
- Designed the user interface
- Applied background colors
- Applied borders
- Resized rows and columns
- Added test values
- Applied text formatting
- Merged cells
- Added moon phase icons
- Added a company logo
- Added controls
- Created a table for non-recurring custom events
- Created a table for recurring custom events
- Packaged the user interface for review by users

important

Update Channels

Update channels determine *when* users will receive the latest Excel version.

Excel 2019 perpetual users

If you have a perpetual license (the pay-once version of Excel 2019) you will not receive any feature updates, so you do not have an update channel.

Excel 365 home users

If you have a subscription version of Excel 2019 (this is referred to as *Excel 365* in this book) that is targeted at home users, you are required to receive monthly updates.

This is called the *Monthly Channel*.

You will potentially receive new or improved features every month.

Excel 365 business users

New features added in the *Monthly Channel* may have bugs, as they will not yet have been extensively tested by real-world use.

If you have an Excel 365 version that is targeted at business users (usually called *Excel Pro Plus*), you will (by default) use the *Semi-annual Update Channel*.

The Semi-annual Channel allows new features to be thoroughly tested before use. It is possible (though difficult) for Excel Pro-Plus users to change their update channel to the *Monthly Channel*.

The *Semi-annual Channel* only updates Excel twice each year (in January and July).

This book was written using *Excel Semi-Annual Version 1808*. This version was released to *Monthly Channel* users on *Jul 24, 2018* and was released to *Semi-Annual* channel users on *Jan 01 2019*.

Lesson 2-1: Check that your Excel version is up to date

Automatic Updates

Normally Excel will look after updates without you having to do anything. By default, automatic updates are enabled. This means that updates are downloaded from the Internet and installed automatically.

It is possible that automatic updates have been switched off on your computer. In this case there is a danger that you may have an old, buggy, unsupported and out of date version of Excel installed.

This lesson will show you how to make sure that you are using the latest (most complete, and most reliable) version of Excel.

1　Start Excel and open a new blank workbook (if you have not already done this).

2　Make sure that automatic updates are enabled.

   1.　Click the *File* button ▭ **File** at the top-left of the screen.

     This takes you to *Backstage View*. Backstage View allows you to complete an enormous range of common tasks from a single window.

   2.　Click: *Account* ▭ **Account** in the left-hand list.

     Your account details are displayed on screen. Notice the *Office Updates* button displayed in the right-hand pane.

     If all is well, and automatic updates are switched on, you will see a button similar to this:

     If *automatic updates* have been switched off, you will see a similar button to this.

     In this case you will need to switch automatic updates on (see next step).

3　Switch on automatic updates if necessary.

     Click: Update Options→Enable Updates.

note

Version number and Build

A new Excel version is usually released to the monthly update channel every month.

Each new version may add new features to Excel 365.

If bugs or security issues are found in a new version, Microsoft will fix them and publish a new *build* of the same version.

It is quite normal for there to be several new *builds* of each new *version* during the month that it is released.

4   If there are updates waiting to install, apply them.

Sometimes Excel will download updates but will not install them automatically.

In this case you will see an update button similar to the following:

If you see this type of button you should apply the update.

Click: Update Options→Apply Updates.

You may be asked to confirm that you want to apply the update, and to close any open programs to apply the update.

5   Notice your version number and update channel.

note

Perpetual license versions have different features

Perpetual license holders still receive monthly updates, but these only include security updates and bug fixes (not new features).

A perpetual license holder running Version 1808 will thus see different features than a subscription license holder running the same Excel version.

You will see a product information section displayed. If you see the number *365* or the words *Subscription Product*, you will know that you are using the subscription version of Excel 2019 (this is the case for products B and C above). Otherwise you are using the *perpetual license* version (this is the case for product A above). In this book, the perpetual license version will be referred to as *Excel 2019* and the subscription version as *Excel 365*.

Notice also the *update channel* and *version numbers* (see sidebars).

6   Click the *Back* button ⬅ to leave *Backstage View* and return to the worksheet.

7   Click the *Close* button ⊠ in the top-right corner of the Excel screen to close Excel.

Lesson 2-2: Design the user interface

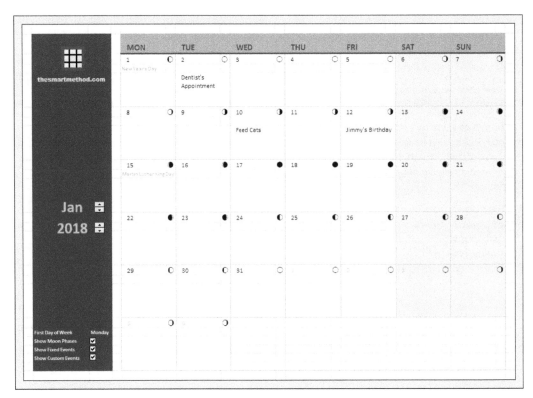

After reviewing the *Functional Specification* described in: *Lesson 1-3: The Functional Specification*, it is possible to identify several design-related constraints that must be satisfied. They are:

1. Show an entire month of dates and events.

2. Allow the user to quickly select any year or month.

3. Allow the user to select Sunday or Monday as the first day of the week.

4. Show the phase of the moon for each date.

5. Allow one fixed event (such as Christmas Day or New Year's Day) to be displayed for each date.

6. Display custom events defined by the user for each date (such as appointments or birthdays). It must be possible to display custom events that are up to 32 characters (in total) long for each day without scrolling.

7. It must be possible to show or hide Moon Phases, Fixed Events and Custom Events.

8. Ensure that the finished calendar looks professional when printed upon one sheet of Letter-Sized or A4 paper (in landscape orientation).

9. The calendar must show 37 days, starting with the Monday or Sunday on or before the 1st of the month that is being displayed.

It is important to appreciate that graphic design and technical implementation are different skills. For this reason, you might decide to use a graphic artist to create the final design.

For the purposes of this lesson, imagine that your designer has submitted the design (shown at the start of this lesson) for approval. You have checked it against the design constraints and decided that it is capable of delivering the functionality required.

You now need to re-create the design within Excel.

The calendar presents a complex user interface that will require information to appear in many different places. To make this possible, each area where a different piece of information will appear needs to be a distinct cell.

For example, above each day in the calendar you need to show the day number and an icon indicating the phase of the moon. In order to do this in Excel, you will need one cell for the day number and another cell for the moon phase.

A designer will usually create a layout using guides (that are normally hidden when the design is printed out). In this case, the designer has provided you with a copy of the design with visible guides (used by the designer to align each item). The guides resemble the rows and columns that appear upon an Excel worksheet. Here is the user interface design with guides:

As you can see, the design will require 21 columns and 26 rows.

You'll begin by applying background colors to define each part of the calendar, then you'll resize the rows and columns, add borders, merge cells as necessary and finally populate cells with test values.

note

The RGB color model

In the 18th century scientists discovered that the human eye had three types of color-sensing cells (called cone cells).

Interestingly, birds and fish have four cone cells (meaning that they can see more colors than humans) and dogs only have two.

The human eye can determine around ten million different colors.

Most computers use an RGB model called *True Color*.

True Color mixes 256 different shades of Red, Green and Blue together to define a color. This means that a computer can display 16 million different colors (more than the human eye can see).

Many corporations have their own "corporate colors" that enable customers to quickly recognize their brand.

In this lesson you define a color that we'll refer to as *Smart Method Indigo*. This is one of the colors used in the Smart Method logo.

Smart Method Indigo can be created by adding 36 parts of Red to 34 parts of Green and 99 parts of Blue.

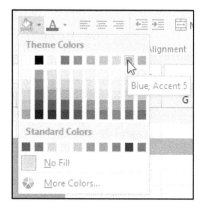

Lesson 2-3: Apply background colors

You know from the design concept which colors that will be used in this project. One of the colors is The Smart Method's corporate Indigo background (used on their web site and some book covers). This color does not exist in any of Excel's built-in color sets, so it is best practice to define it as a custom color by specifying the RGB (Red, Green and Blue) components.

1   Open Excel and create a new blank workbook.

2   Select all cells and apply a gray background color.

   1.   Select all cells, either by clicking the Select All button ☐ (or by using the **<Ctrl>+<A>** keyboard shortcut.

   2.   Click: Home→Font→Fill Color.

   3.   Apply the *Light Gray, Background 2* fill color (the 3rd color from the left on the top row of colors).

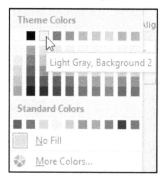

3   Select cells B2:T25 and apply the *No Fill* background color.

These are the cells that will contain the calendar.

4   Select cells F3:S3 and apply the *Orange-Accent 2* background color (the orange color on the top row).

These are the cells that will contain the names of each day of the week.

5   Select cells C3:D24 and apply the *Blue-Accent 5* background color (the second color from the right on the top row).

Excel's default color set doesn't include the indigo color used in the design specification. The nearest is *Blue-Accent 5* but that isn't an exact match.

You could define the correct color using the *More Colors* option, but this would prevent the colors from automatically changing if the user changed the theme.

To enable themes to work correctly, you'll select the *Accent 5* color and change *Accent 5* in this workbook's *Color Set* to the indigo color that you need.

6   Customize the workbook's Color Set so that the Accent 5 color matches the indigo color in the specification.

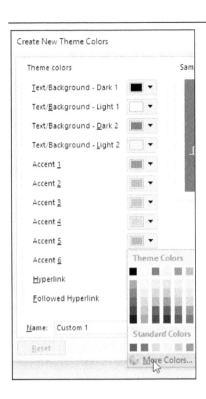

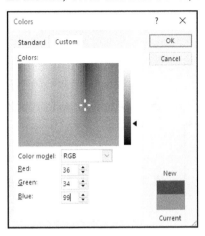

1. Click: Page Layout→Themes→Colors→Customize Colors.

2. Click: Accent 5→More Colors.

3. In the *Red*, *Green* and *Blue* boxes, enter the values **36**, **34** and **99**.

4. Click: *OK*.

5. In the *Name* box, enter: **Year Planner Color Set**

6. Click: *Save*.

Cells C3:D24 change to the correct color.

You can now see a very basic outline of the calendar. In the next lesson, you'll add borders according to the design concept.

You'll notice that you didn't add shading for weekends. This is because the calendar needs to be able to work with either Monday or Sunday as the start of the week, meaning that the shaded weekend area will move according to the settings.

You'll apply the weekend shading using Conditional Formatting later, in: *Lesson 3-10: Add conditional formatting for weekends.*

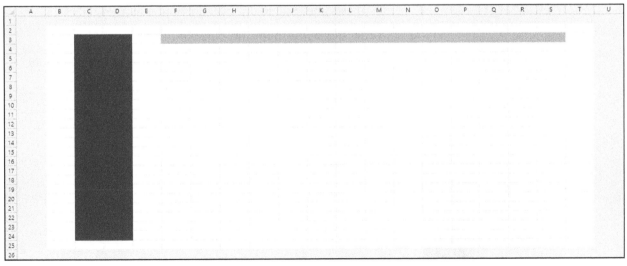

7. Save the workbook as *Year Planner-1*.

Lesson 2-4: Apply borders

1 Open *Year Planner-1* (if it isn't already open).

2 Switch off gridlines.

Click: View→Show→Gridlines.

Switching off the gridlines makes it easier to see the borders that you are going to apply.

3 Apply a solid black border around cells B2:T25.

1. Select cells B2:T25.

2. Click: Home→Font→Borders→Outside Borders.

4 Apply a gray border around cells F4:S24.

1. Select cells F4:S24.

2. Click: Home→Font→Borders→Line Color and select the *White, Background 1, Darker 25%* color (the 4th from the top on the left-most column).

The cursor changes into a pencil [✏], indicating that you are in border-drawing mode.

3. Click and drag to draw a gray border around cells F4:S24.

5 Draw the borders for the calendar cells.

Click and drag to draw the remaining borders for the calendar cells, so that the workbook looks like this:

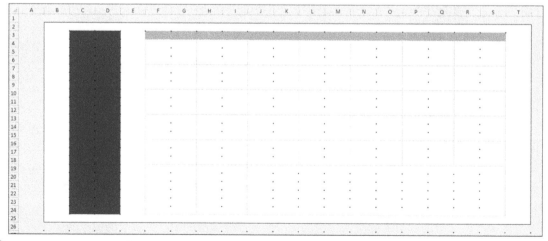

6 Press **<Escape>** to exit border-drawing mode.

Year Planner-1

7 Apply a dark blue border to the bottom of cells F3:S3.

1. Select cells F3:S3.

2. Right click the selected cells and click *Format Cells* from the shortcut menu.

3. Click the *Border* tab.

4. Select the thickest solid border style and the new *Indigo, Accent 5* custom color that you created in: *Lesson 2-3: Apply background colors.*

5. Click the button indicating a bottom border and click OK.

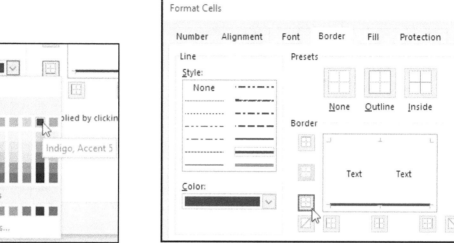

With the borders in place, the framework of the calendar is now much more obvious.

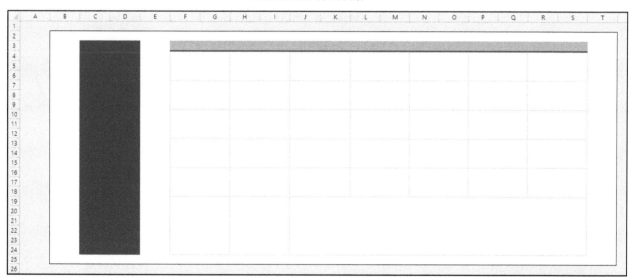

In the next lesson you'll resize the rows and columns so that they are the same size as those shown in the design concept.

8   Save the workbook as *Year Planner-2*.

Lesson 2-5: Resize rows and columns

1 Open *Year Planner-2* (if it isn't already open).

2 Resize the columns according to the specification.

    1. Select columns B, E, G, I, K, M, O, Q, S and T.

       To do this, hold down the **<Ctrl>** key on your keyboard and click each column heading.

    2. Click and drag the edge of any of the selected column headings to resize all of the selected columns to be *20 pixels* wide.

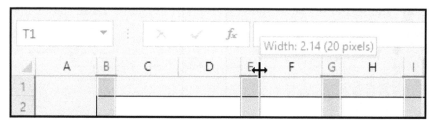

    3. Select columns F, H, J, L, N, P and R and resize them to be *93 pixels* wide.

    4. Resize column C to be *117 pixels* wide.

    5. Resize column D to be *48 pixels* wide.

    6. Resize columns A and U to be *17 pixels* wide.

The columns are now all the correct size.

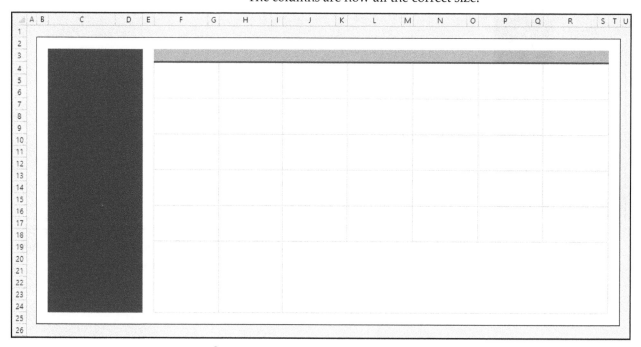

3 Resize the rows according to the specification.

    1. Resize row 3 to be *39 pixels* high.

Year Planner-2

You can resize rows in almost the same way as you resized columns. Click and drag the edge of row 3 to resize the row to *39 pixels*.

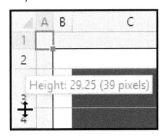

2. Resize rows 6, 9, 12, 15 and 18 to be *68 pixels* high.

   Resizing multiple rows is the same as resizing multiple columns. Hold down the **<Ctrl>** key and then click on each row number to select them. You can then resize them all at the same size by resizing any of the selected rows.

3. Resize rows 1, 5, 8, 11, 14, 17, 20, 21, 22, 23, 24 and 26 to be *17 pixels* high.

The calendar's appearance now perfectly matches the design specification. In the next lesson, you'll add some test values to the calendar's cells to match the design brief.

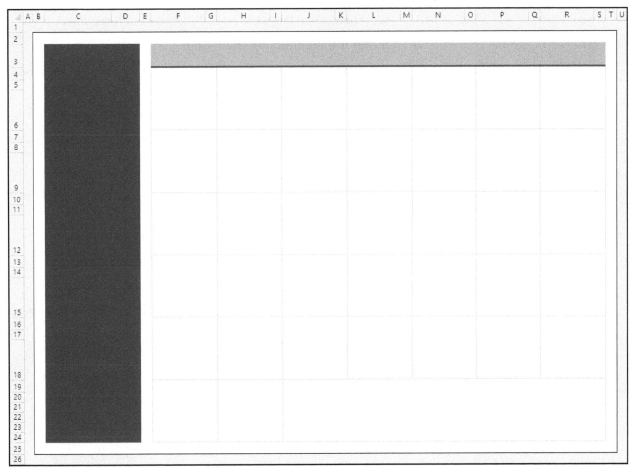

4   Save the workbook as *Year Planner-3*.

Lesson 2-6: Add test values

Before making the calendar functional, you're going to add some test values to the cells. This will enable you to make sure that the values appear in the right places and confirm that the formatting is correct.

1   Open *Year Planner-3* (if it isn't already open).

2   Add the week days to row 3.

   1.   Click in cell F3 and type the text: **MON**

   2.   Select cells F3:G3 and then AutoFill across to cell S3.

To AutoFill across, click and drag the *fill handle* on the bottom-right corner of the selected cells.

Because you've selected both the cell containing MON and the blank cell next to it, Excel is able to figure out that you want to leave a blank cell between each day of the week.

Don't worry about the formatting of the text for now. You'll change that later, in: *Lesson 2-7: Apply text formatting*.

3   Enter the numbers for each date.

For testing purposes, you're going to enter the dates for the month of January 2016.

   1.   Enter the numbers **28**, **29**, **30** and **31** in cells F4, H4, J4 and L4.

As shown in the design concept, the calendar will always show 37 days, showing the dates from the next or previous months wherever they overlap.

These numbers represent the 28th to 31st of December 2015 to match the dates shown in the design.

   2.   Enter the numbers **1**, **2**, and **3** in cells N4, P4 and R4.

These represent the 1st, 2nd and 3rd of January 2016.

   3.   In the same columns on row 7, enter the numbers **4-10**.

You can use AutoFill to speed this up in the same way as you did with the days of the week.

   4.   In the same columns on row 10, enter the numbers **11-17**.

   5.   In the same columns on row 13, enter the numbers **18-24**.

   6.   In the same columns on row 16, enter the numbers **25-31**.

   7.   Enter the numbers **1** and **2** in cells F19 and H19.

These represent the 1st and 2nd of February 2016.

All of the numbers are now in place. You'll notice that they're not aligned or formatted correctly. You'll change that later, in: *Lesson 2-7: Apply text formatting*.

4   Enter some fixed events.

Year Planner-3

1. Enter **New Year's Day** in cell N5.

   Cell N5 is below the cell indicating the 1st of January 2016.

2. Enter **Martin Luther King Day** in cell F14.

   Cell F14 is below the cell indicating the 18th of January 2016.

5 Enter some custom events.

   1. Type: **Dentist's Appointment** in cell P6.

   2. Type: **Feed Cats** in cell R9.

   3. Type: **Jimmy's Birthday** in cell H12.

6 Enter the year and month in cell C11.

   Enter **Jan 2016** in cell C11.

   This will be the wrong color and size and won't be formatted correctly, but for now entering the value is all that is important.

7 Enter the headings for the calendar settings.

   1. Type: **First Day of Week** in cell C20.

   2. Type: **Monday** in cell D20.

   3. Type: **Show Moon Phases** in cell C21.

   4. Type: **Show Fixed Events** in cell C22.

   5. Type: **Show Custom Events** in cell C23.

The calendar is now populated with test data. As you can see, a lot more formatting is needed to match the design concept. You'll apply that formatting in the next lesson. (In the grab below the color of the left-hand bar has been lightened so that you can see the text entered).

note

If the text is hard to read

The text that you enter in steps 6 and 7 might be hard to read, as it will be black text on a very dark indigo background.

If this is a problem for you, temporarily change the background color of the cells to a lighter color. You'll reformat the text to make it easier to read on a dark background in the next lesson, so you should change the color back at that point.

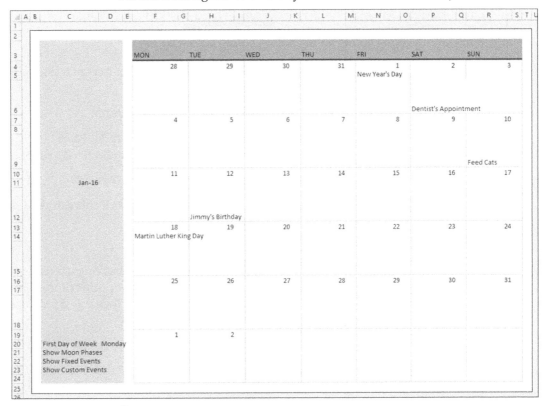

8 Save the workbook as *Year Planner-4*.

Lesson 2-7: Apply text formatting

1   Open *Year Planner-4* (if it isn't already open).

2   Align the dates to the left.

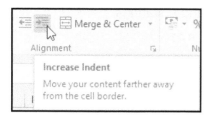

If you look at the design concept, you'll see that the date numbers are supposed to be left-aligned. They are currently right-aligned because that is Excel's default for numeric values.

1. Select cells F3:S24.

2. Click: Home→Alignment→Align Left.

   All of the selected cells are now left aligned.

3   Apply a left indent to cells F3:S24.

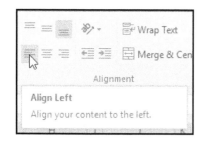

The design concept shows that all of the values in the calendar are slightly indented from the left. You can apply this to your calendar using Excel's *Alignment* features.

1. Select cells F3:S24 (if they're not still selected).

2. Click: Home→Alignment→Increase Indent.

The week days, events and date numbers are all slightly indented.

4   Set the font size of cells F4:S24 to **10 points**.

5   Set the font style for the week day names.

1. Select cells F3:S3.

2. Set the font size to **13 points** (you will have to type this into the font size box).

3. Make the text bold.

4. Set the font color to **Indigo, Accent 5** (the same as the blue sidebar).

6   Set the font style for fixed events.

1. Select cells F5:S5, F8:S8, F11:S11, F14:S14, F17:S17 and F20:I20 (all of the cells that will contain fixed events).

2. Set the font color to **Green, Accent 6**.

3. Click: Home→Alignment→Decrease Indent to remove the indent from fixed events.

4. Set the font size to **8 points**.

   Martin Luther King Day is the widest fixed event that is specified in the Functional Specification. A font size of 8 points (in the Calibri font) is thus the largest font size that can be used.

7   Set the font style for custom events.

1. Select cells F6:S6, F9:S9, F12:S12, F15:S15, F18:S18 and F21:I21 (all of the cells that will contain custom events).

Year Planner-4

2. Click: Home→Alignment→Top Align to display all of the custom events at the top of their cells instead of at the bottom.

3. Click: Home→Alignment→Wrap Text to prevent custom events from overflowing their cells.

8 **Set the font style for the year and month.**

1. Select cell C11.

2. Set the font size to **24 points**.

3. Make the text bold.

4. Set the font color to **Gold, Accent 4**.

5. Set the vertical alignment to **Middle Align** and the horizontal alignment to **Center**.

6. Click: *Wrap Text* to enable text wrapping.

The text is too big to fit in cell C11, so it will be cut off in the display. You'll fix this later, in: *Lesson 2-8: Merge cells,* by merging cell C11 with other nearby cells.

9 **Set the font style for the settings.**

1. Select cells C20:D23 (the cells where the calendar settings are displayed).

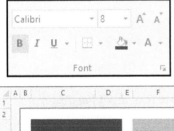

2. Set the font size to **8 points**.

3. Make the text bold.

4. Set the font color to **White**.

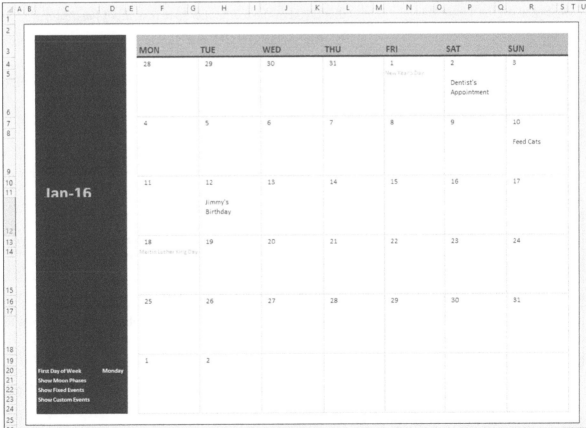

10 Save the workbook as *Year Planner-5.*

tip

Speeding up merging cells

The *Merge Cells* command is a little awkward to access, since you have to open the *Merge & Center* dropdown menu every time you want to use it.

You can make it quicker to access by adding it to your *Quick Access Toolbar*. To do this, right-click on the *Merge Cells* command and click *Add to Quick Access Toolbar* from the shortcut menu.

You can now merge cells with one click instead of two.

Adding a command to your Quick Access Toolbar also automatically creates a keyboard shortcut. The first item on your Quick Access Toolbar can be accessed using <Alt>+<1>, the second with <Alt>+<2>, and so on. This allows you to quickly merge and center cells without needing to use the mouse at all.

Lesson 2-8: Merge cells

All of the formatting is now correct, but some of the cells need to be merged. The text indicating the year and month needs a lot of screen space, so you'll merge several cells into one larger cell to give it more room.

There are also several other cells that should be merged to increase the amount of information that can be displayed in each part of the calendar.

1   Open *Year Planner-5* (if it isn't already open).

2   Switch gridlines on.

Click: View→Show→Gridlines to display the gridlines (if they're not already visible).

The gridlines will make it easier to see where cells have been merged.

3   Merge & Center cells C11:D15.

1. Select cells C11:D15.

2. Click: Home→Alignment→Merge & Center.

The year and month are no longer cut off, as they now have space to be fully displayed.

4   Set the format for the year and month.

Now that the year and month are fully visible, you can see that they don't quite match the design concept. They should be displayed in the format *Jan 2016* instead of *Jan-16*.

1. Right-click cell C11 and click *Format Cells* from the shortcut menu.

2. Click the *Number* tab (if it isn't already selected) and click *Custom* from the left-hand list.

3. In the *Type* box, enter: **mmm**

4. Still in the *Type* box, press <Ctrl>+<J>.

    This is a (very little known) way of entering a line break within a custom format.

5. Finish the custom format with: **yyyy**

    You won't be able to see this text as you type it, but you will see the year appear in the *Sample* box above.

6. Click: OK.

The year and month are now displayed correctly. If the line break between the year and month isn't visible, it's because you forgot to switch on *Wrap Text* for cell C11 in the previous lesson.

5   Merge the cells for custom events.

If you look at the cells that contain custom events, you'll notice that there is an extra cell to the right of each event.

You can see that the fixed events, such as *Martin Luther King Day* aren't bothered by this because they're able to overflow into the

Year Planner-5

cell to the right. However, *Wrap Text* has been enabled for the cells containing custom events, preventing them from overflowing into the next cell.

In order to give custom events as much space as possible, you need to merge each custom event cell with the cell to the right.

1. Select cells F6:G6.

2. Click: Home→Alignment→
    Merge & Center Dropdown→Merge Cells.

3. Repeat the process for cells H6:I6, J6:K6, L6:M6, N6:O6, P6:Q6 and R6:S6.

    The first row of custom events should now look like this:

MON	TUE	WED	THU	FRI	SAT	SUN
28	29	30	31	1 New Year's Day	2 Dentist's Appointment	3

4. Repeat the process for rows 9, 12, 15 and 18.

    The last two days are a little different, because you have had to add several extra rows to make room for the calendar settings. All this means is that you will have to merge a few more cells for the last two days.

5. Merge cells F21:G24 and H21:I24.

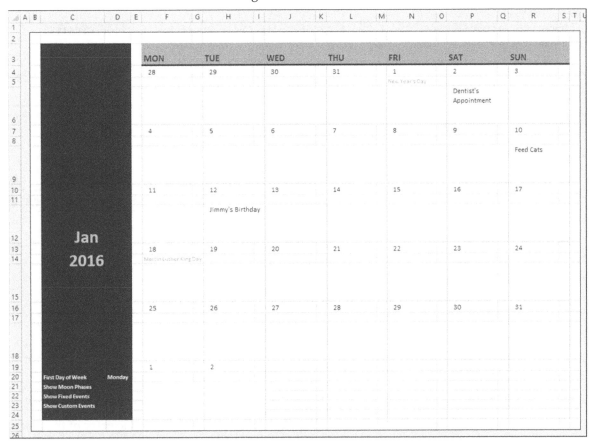

6   Save the workbook as *Year Planner-6*.

Lesson 2-9: Add moon phase symbols

note

Getting more symbols

The symbols that are available via the *Symbols* dialog are provided by the fonts installed on your computer. In this lesson you're using the *Segoe UI Symbol* font, which has been automatically included with every copy of Office (since Office 2007) and Windows (since Windows Vista).

If you need more symbols, you can download additional fonts from the Internet.

Always remember, however, that custom fonts won't be available on other people's computers. If you send a workbook to someone that doesn't have the same fonts as you, they won't see your custom symbols.

For this reason, it's a good idea to stay with the fonts that are provided with Windows unless you are the only user of the workbook.

note

The new Segoe Emoji font

Segoe UI Symbol was the default icon font in Excel 2016. With the release of Excel 2019 Microsoft have added the *Segoe UI Emoji* font, which is intended to replace *Segoe UI* for many symbols, including the moon phases used in this lesson.

If you prefer the look of the symbols in the *Segoe UI Emoji* font, you can use it instead of *Segoe UI Symbol*.

Year Planner-6

The next things you'll add to your user interface are the symbols for the moon phases. Later you'll make them automatically change according to the date.

It isn't possible to make photographic images appear and disappear using an Excel formula. The solution is to use one of the many special symbols that are available in Microsoft Office's built-in library of fonts. It will then be possible for an Excel formula to make any of these symbols appear in a cell.

1   Open *Year Planner-6* (if it isn't already open).

2   Add a 'new moon' symbol to cell G4.

    1.   Select cell G4.

    2.   Click: Insert→Symbols→Symbol.

        The *Symbol* dialog appears.

    3.   Click the *Font* dropdown and select the *Segoe UI Symbol* font.

        You can now see the huge number of symbols that are available. There are over 5000 different symbols in this font, so it could take a very long time to find the ones you need by scrolling through the list. Fortunately, you can take a shortcut to the right place.

    4.   Click in the *Character code* box and enter: **1F311**

        You are instantly teleported to the *New Moon Symbol* entry, which is highlighted near the top of the window. You can also see the other moon symbols nearby.

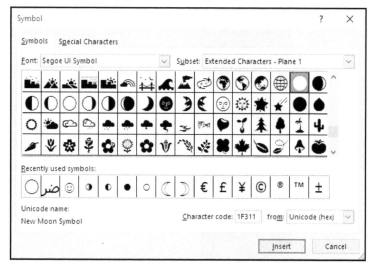

    5.   Click: *Insert* to insert the new moon symbol.

    6.   Close the *Symbol* dialog by clicking the *Close* button.

    7.   Press the **<Enter>** key to confirm the entry of the new moon symbol.

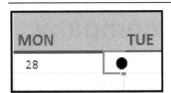

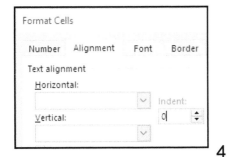

The new moon symbol appears in cell G3, but it doesn't look quite right. This is because it has picked up the indentation that you added in: *Lesson 2-7: Apply text formatting*.

3   Remove the indent from the moon symbol cells.

1.   Select columns G, I, K, M, O, Q and S.

2.   Right click one of the selected column headers and click: *Format Cells…* from the shortcut menu.

3.   Click the *Alignment* tab.

4.   In the *Indent* box, type: **0**

5.   Click: *OK*.

     The indent disappears.

4   Add symbols for the other moon phases.

Use the same process to add moon symbols to every day on the calendar. When you get to the *Waning Crescent Moon Symbol*, start again with the *New Moon Symbol* for the next day.

There's no need to keep going back to the *Symbol* dialog after you have inserted the first set of symbols. You can simply copy and paste them once they're on the workbook.

The moon phase doesn't change every day in real life of course, but this will be a good way of confirming that everything is formatted correctly.

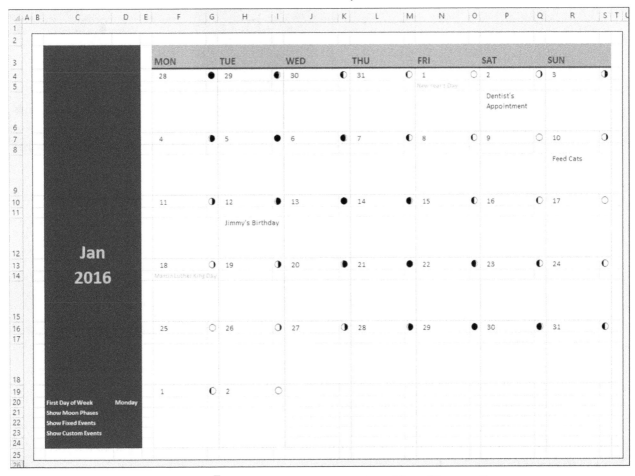

5   Save the workbook as *Year Planner-7*.

Lesson 2-10: Add a company logo

The design concept shows a company logo in the top-left corner of the calendar. You'll add the logo in this lesson.

1 Open *Year Planner-7* (if it isn't already open).

2 Insert the Smart Method logo in cells C3:D6.

1. Select cells C3:D6.

2. Click: Insert→Illustrations→Pictures.

3. Navigate to your sample files folder and click *thesmartmethod.png*.

4. Click *Insert*.

   The Smart Method logo appears on your workbook.

5. Click and drag to move the logo to the top-left corner of the workbook.

6. Click and drag the sizing handles to resize the logo as needed.

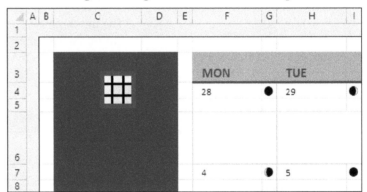

3 Insert a text box containing the text **thesmartmethod.com**

1. Click: Insert→Text→Text Box.

2. Click below the Smart Method logo to insert a new text box.

   Be careful not to click and drag as this will insert a text box with a background color and border that you'd need to remove.

3. Type: **thesmartmethod.com**

4. Click and drag to select the text that you have entered.

   Alternatively, press **<Ctrl> + <A>** to select all text in the text box.

5. Use the options in the Home→Font group to make the text **Arial Black**, size **9**, **bold**.

6. Set the font color to the standard color: **Yellow**

Year Planner-7

note

Standard colors are not compatible with themes

You might have noticed that you're using a color from the *Standard Colors* set in this lesson, rather than the *Theme Colors* set.

This means that the color won't change if the workbook's theme is changed, potentially making the text hard to read.

You've done this because the image above the text is also yellow and images can't change their colors to match the selected theme.

If the workbook's theme made the company logo difficult to see, it would be necessary to either create a new logo image or change the theme to a more appropriate color scheme.

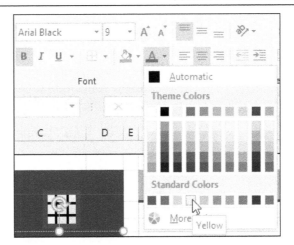

7. Click and drag one of the edges of the text box to move it into position below the Smart Method logo.

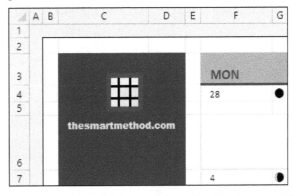

You've now added the logo to the calendar. You could replace this with your own company logo or any other image.

4   Save the workbook as *Year Planner-8*.

Lesson 2-11: Add controls

Although you're creating a non-functional user interface, it's still useful to add the controls that the user will use to change the calendar's settings. This makes it clear how the user interface works.

1   Open *Year Planner-8* (if it isn't already open).

2   Enable the *Developer* tab if it isn't already visible.

    1.   Right-click any of the Ribbon tabs (except the *File* tab) and click *Customize the Ribbon* from the shortcut menu.

    2.   In the right-hand pane, click the *Developer* checkbox.

    3.   Click *OK*.

3   Add Spin Button form controls to change the month and year.

    1.   Click: Developer→Controls→Insert→Spin Button (Form Control).

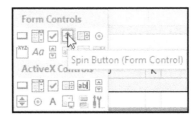

It's important to select the spin button from the *Form Controls* section and not the *ActiveX Controls* section.

    2.   Click near the word *Jan* to create a spin button.

    3.   Right-click the spin button and click *Format Control* from the shortcut menu.

    4.   Click the *Size* tab and set the *Height* and *Width* settings to: **0.5**

    5.   Click *OK*.

Year Planner-8

tip

Perfectly aligning form controls

To align the check boxes perfectly you can use this technique:

1. Right-click a Check Box control to select it.

2. Hold down the **<Shift>** key and right-click on each of the other two Check Box controls so that all three are selected.

3. Click:

Drawing Tools→Format→ Arrange→Align→Align Left

You can see that there are also many other alignment options.

6. Drag the spin button into position next to the word *Jan*.

   If you can't move the spin button, remember that you need to right-click on it to select it so that it can be moved.

7. Use Copy and Paste to create a copy of the spin button and drag it into position next to *2016*.

4 **Add Check Box controls for the three check box settings**.

1. Click: Developer→Controls→Insert→ Check Box (Form Control).

2. Click near the words *Show Moon Phases* to create a check box.

3. Right-click the new check box and click *Edit Text* from the shortcut menu.

4. Delete all text from the check box.

5. Drag the check box into place next to *Show Moon Phases*.

6. Copy and paste the check box and place the copy next to *Show Fixed Events*.

7. Copy and paste the check box again and place the copy next to *Show Custom Events*.

5 **Switch off gridlines**.

Hiding the gridlines will make it easier to confirm that everything is correct.

Click: View→Show→Gridlines.

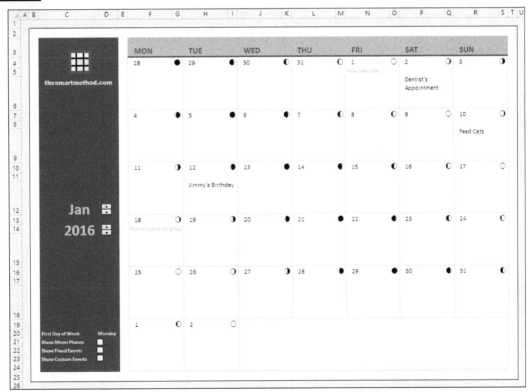

The calendar interface is now fully defined. None of the controls are functional yet, but you can see exactly how it will work and where all of the information will appear.

6 Save the workbook as *Year Planner-9*.

Lesson 2-12: Create a table for non-recurring custom events

The calendar user interface is fully defined, but you still haven't defined the interface for entering the events that will appear on the calendar.

There are two types of events: events that only happen once and events that recur on the same date every year. You're going to define a table to enter non-recurring events in this lesson.

1   Open *Year Planner-9* (if it isn't already open).

2   Add a new worksheet named **Custom Events**.

    1.   Click the *New sheet* icon below the worksheet: ⊕

        A new worksheet named *Sheet2* appears.

    2.   Right click the *Sheet2* worksheet and click *Rename* from the shortcut menu.

    3.   Type **Custom Events** and press <**Enter**>.

3   Rename the *Sheet1* worksheet to **Calendar**.

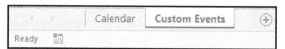

4   Select the *Custom Events* worksheet if it isn't already selected.

5   In cell A1, type: **Custom Events**

6   Apply the *Title* style to cell A1.

    1.   Select cell A1.

    2.   Click: Home→Styles→Cell Styles Gallery→Title.

7   Merge cells A3:B3.

    1.   Select cells A3:B3.

    2.   Click: Home→Alignment→Merge & Center (Drop-down)→Merge Cells.

8   In cell A3, type: **Non-Recurring**

9   Apply the *Heading 2* style to cell A3.

    1.   Select cell A3.

    2.   Click: Home→Styles→Cell Styles Gallery→Heading 2.

10   Enter data for non-recurring custom events.

Enter the following data into cells A5:B7, resizing the columns as needed:

Year Planner-9

11 Define the custom events data as a Table.

1. Select cells A5:B7.

2. Click: Insert→Tables→Table.

3. Click: *OK* when prompted.

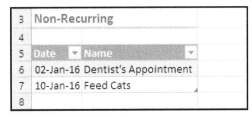

The colors change, and filter arrows appear, indicating that a Table has been defined. This Table is the area where users will input the custom events that need to appear in the calendar.

Because it's been defined as a Table, the Calendar's formulas will be able to work with its contents even if rows are added or removed (see sidebar).

12 Set the name of the Table to: **CustomEvents**

1. Click anywhere in the Table.

2. Click: Table Tools→Design→Properties→Table Name.

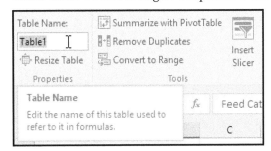

3. Type **CustomEvents** and press <Enter>.

You've now named your table so that it can be easily accessed by the formulas that you will create later.

13 Resize the table so that each column is wide enough to fully display the contents.

1. Select cells A5:B7.

2. Click: Home→Cells→Format→AutoFit Column Width.

The column widths are perfectly sized.

14 Save the workbook as *Year Planner-10*.

Lesson 2-13: Create a table for recurring custom events

Recurring events are events such as birthdays that recur on the same date every year. In this lesson you'll add a table to enable the user to define recurring events.

1 Open *Year Planner-10* (if it isn't already open).

2 Select the *Custom Events* worksheet if it isn't already selected.

3 Merge cells D3:E3.

4 In cell D3, type: **Recurring**

5 Apply the *Heading 2* style to cell D3.

6 Enter data for recurring custom events in cells D5:E6 and re-size columns D and E as needed.

7 Define the custom events data as a Table.

1. Select cells D5:E6.

2. Click: Insert→Tables→Table.

3. Click: *OK* when prompted.

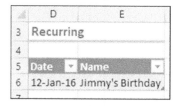

The colors change and filter arrows appear, indicating that a Table has been defined. This Table is the area where users will input recurring custom events that need to appear in the calendar.

Because it's been defined as a Table, the calendar's formulas will be able to work with the table's contents even if rows are added or removed.

8 Set the name of the Table to: **RecurringEvents**

1. Click anywhere in the Table.

2. Click: Table Tools→Design→Properties→Table Name.

Year Planner-10

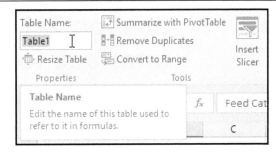

3. Type **RecurringEvents** and press **<Enter>**.

You've now named your table so that it can be easily accessed by the formulas that you will create later.

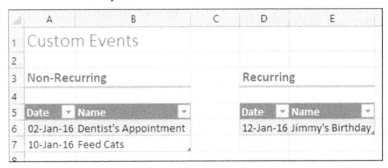

The user interface is now complete. All of the areas where users will enter data have been defined.

9 Save the workbook as *Year Planner-11*.

Year Planner-11

Lesson 2-14: Package the user interface for review by users

You've now completed the user interface.

Your users have already signed off on the functional specification that defined each feature the application had to deliver.

Because the user interface is non-functional it is important to convey to users what each of the controls will do in the finished application. You'll do this by adding callouts.

The user interface can then be circulated amongst end users for feedback.

1 Open *Year Planner-11* (if it isn't already open).

2 Select the *Calendar* worksheet.

3 Add a white oval speech bubble shape to the right of the month shown in the indigo sidebar.

1. Click: Insert→Illustrations→Shapes→Callouts→ Speech Bubble: Oval.

2. Click to the right of the date shown in the left-hand indigo sidebar.

   An oval speech bubble appears.

3. Make sure that the speech bubble is selected.

4. Click: Drawing Tools→Format→ Shape Styles Gallery→Theme Styles→ Colored Outline – Black, Dark 1

   This is the first style and is shown on the top left of the gallery.

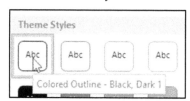

4 Resize and position the Speech Bubble and add text so that it looks like this:

1. Click on the Speech Bubble to select it and click and drag any of the sizing handles to re-size. You can also use the yellow handle to size and re-position the Speech Bubble's arrow.

2. Click in an empty part of the Speech Bubble until you see the four-headed arrow cursor shape and then drag to re-position.

3. Right-click in an empty part of the Speech Bubble and select: *Edit Text* from the shortcut menu to edit the text within the Speech Bubble.

5   Add speech bubbles to other calendar elements to illustrate how each of the features described in the functional specification will be delivered.

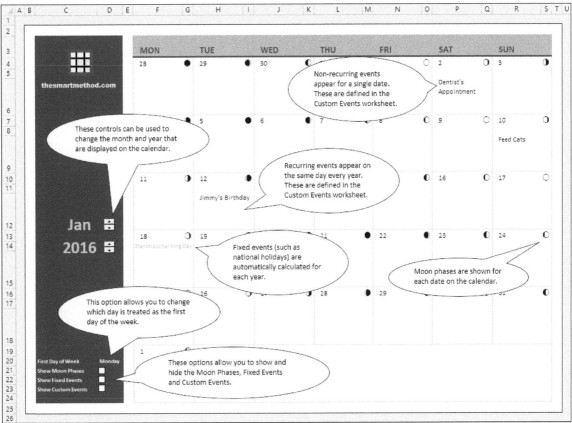

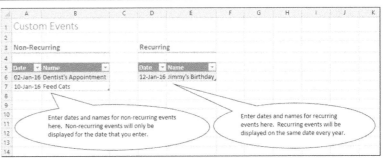

note

Managing users' expectations

It is useful to circulate the user interface for two reasons:

1. Users often spot a feature that was missed at the functional specification phase.

2. Your users are given advance notification of how the finished application will look.

Having defined and approved both the functionality and user interface there will be no surprises when you deliver the application. Your project will then be considered a success.

6   Protect both worksheets to prevent users from accidentally making changes to them.

1. Select the *Calendar* worksheet.

2. Click: Review→Protect→Protect Sheet.

3. Select the *Custom Events* worksheet.

4. Click Review→Protect→Protect Sheet.

In Excel 2016, the *Protect* Ribbon group was called *Changes*.

7   Save the workbook as *User Interface Specification Version 1*.

Blank page

3

Session Three: Make the calendar functional

> It's important to have a sound idea, but the really important thing is the implementation.
>
> *Wilbur Ross, American investor and government official (b 1937)*

The non-functional prototype of the calendar is now complete.

In this session you'll make the prototype functional as a calendar.

You'll put more advanced features such as the events and moon phases on hold for now and concentrate on making the calendar display the correct dates for the selected year and month.

Session Objectives

By the end of this session you will have:

- Created placeholders for calendar control settings
- Defined range names for the calendar control settings
- Made the first day of week selector functional
- Set control cell links
- Created helper cells to determine the calendar start date
- Created formulas to determine the calendar start date
- Created formulas to display each date on the calendar
- Created formulas to display the days of the week
- Added conditional formatting to the day numbers
- Added conditional formatting for weekends
- Added conditional formatting for the moon phases

Lesson 3-1: Create placeholders for calendar control settings

Control settings will be used to calculate the information that should be displayed by the calendar at any point in time

Control settings can be changed at any time via controls on the user interface. The controls determine:

- The month to display.

- The year to display.

- Whether the first day of the week is a Sunday or a Monday.

- Whether to show or hide the moon phases, fixed events and custom events.

In this lesson you will define placeholders for these six control settings. Later, in: *Lesson 3-3: Make the first day of week selector functional* and *Lesson 3-4: Set control cell links*, you will connect these placeholders to the six controls on the user interface.

1   Open *Year Planner-11* (if it isn't already open).

2   Add placeholders for the calendar date settings.

1. Click the *Calendar* worksheet tab if it isn't already selected.

2. In cell V2, type: **Year**

3. In cell W2, type: **2016**

    This will be the control setting that defines which year is currently displayed in the calendar.

4. In cell V3, type: **Month**

5. In cell W3, type: **1**

    This will be the control setting that defines which month is displayed. The number 1 indicates January.

    Many of Excel's functions require month numbers rather than names. For this reason, it is better to use the number 1 (where 1=January, 2=February etc) than the text: **January** or **Jan**.

6. In cell V4, type: **Week Start Mode**

7. In cell W4, type: **1**

    Cell W4 will contain the control setting that defines whether Monday or Sunday is treated as the first day of the week. The number 1 will indicate that Sunday will be the first day of the week, while the number 2 will indicate Monday.

8. Resize column V so that it is wide enough to show all of its contents.

tip

Quickly resizing columns

You can quickly resize a column to be exactly the right width to display all of its contents.

To do this, move your mouse cursor over the intersection of two columns until you see the double-headed arrow cursor shape:

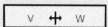

When you see the double-headed arrow, double-click with the mouse to automatically resize the column.

Year Planner-11

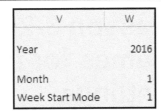

The basic calendar control settings are now defined. With these three control settings alone, you will be able to create the formulas that the calendar will need to display the correct dates for every year.

3   Add placeholders for the three checkbox control settings.

You're not going to make the events or moon phases functional in this session, but you'll create control settings for the checkboxes that determine whether they are displayed in the calendar.

1.   In cell V5, enter: **Show Moon Phases**

2.   In cell W5, type: **TRUE**

3.   In cell V6, type: **Show Fixed Events**

4.   In cell W6, type: **TRUE**

5.   In cell V7, type: **Show Custom Events**

6.   In cell W7, type: **TRUE**

7.   Resize column V again if necessary.

Later, in: *Lesson 3-3: Make the first day of week selector functional* and *Lesson 3-4: Set control cell links,* you will connect the control settings in cells W2:W7 to the six user interface controls on the calendar worksheet.

You will create many formulas in this construction kit that need to reference the control settings to return correct values.

The control settings in columns V and W will be hidden from the user in the final version of the calendar, so their formatting isn't very important.

4   Save the workbook as *Year Planner-12*.

Lesson 3-2: Define range names for the calendar control settings

When you create formulas in Excel, you usually refer to cells using cell references such as =*W4*. This works, but can be confusing as it isn't always clear what the value in cell W4 signifies.

Range names offer an elegant solution, and allow you to create formulas such as =*WeekStartMode*. This makes it clear that you are retrieving the week start mode and makes it much easier to understand the formula and avoid any mistakes.

In this lesson you'll add range names to the control settings that you defined in the previous lesson. This will make them much easier to work with later, when you create formulas that reference the control settings.

1   Open *Year Planner-12* (if it isn't already open).

2   Define a range name for the selected year in cell W2, named: **CalendarYear**

  1. Click in cell W2 to select it.

  2. Click in the *Name Box*.

  The *Name Box* can be found in the top-left corner of the Excel interface. It will currently contain the text *W2*.

  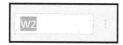

  3. Type **CalendarYear** and press the **<Enter>** key.

  You've now defined cell W2 as the *CalendarYear* range name. This means you can access it by that name in any formula. Range names will make the formulas that you will create later a lot easier to understand.

3   Add range names for the other calendar settings.

  You're going to define range names for each of the other settings in exactly the same way.

  1. Define cell W3 as the **CalendarMonth** range name.

  2. Define cell W4 as the **WeekStartMode** range name.

  3. Define cell W5 as the **ShowMoonPhases** range name.

  4. Define cell W6 as the **ShowFixedEvents** range name.

  5. Define cell W7 as the **ShowCustomEvents** range name.

4   Open the Name Manager and confirm that the range names are correct.

  Click: Formulas→Defined Names→Name Manager.

Year Planner-12

The *Name Manager* window opens, showing the range names that have been defined.

Name	Value	Refers To	Scope	Comment
CalendarMonth	1	=Calendar!$W$3	Workbook	
CalendarYear	2016	=Calendar!$W$2	Workbook	
CustomEvents	{"2-Jan-16","Dentist...	='Custom Events'!$...	Workbook	
RecurringEvents	{"12-Jan-16","Jimmy...	='Custom Events'!$...	Workbook	
ShowCustomEvents	TRUE	=Calendar!$W$7	Workbook	
ShowFixedEvents	TRUE	=Calendar!$W$6	Workbook	
ShowMoonPhases	TRUE	=Calendar!$W$5	Workbook	
WeekStartMode	1	=Calendar!$W$4	Workbook	

You should confirm that your range names are correct before continuing. (They may appear in a different order from the screen grab above).

If any of your range names are incorrect, edit or delete them by clicking on the appropriate range name and then clicking the *Delete* or *Edit* buttons. You can then correct the range name.

5   Save the workbook as *Year Planner-13*.

Lesson 3-3: Make the first day of week selector functional

The functional specification stated:

It must be possible to select either Sunday or Monday as the first day of the week.

You've allowed for the first day of the week to be specified in the user interface. You could allow the user to simply type the day of the week into cell D20 but this would be rather error-prone. In this lesson you'll offer a simple choice between two days via a drop-down list.

1 Open *Year Planner-13* (if it isn't already open).

2 Add a List validation to cell D20 to allow the user to switch between Monday and Sunday as the first day of the week.

A List validation adds a dropdown menu to a cell, enabling the user to select from a list of options.

1. Click in cell D20 to make it the active cell.

2. Click: Data→Data Tools→Data Validation.

3. Click the Settings tab.

4. Click on the *Allow* drop-down menu.

5. Click: *List* from the dropdown menu.

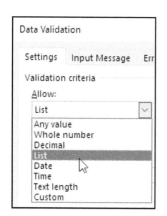

6. Click in the *Source* box and type: **Monday,Sunday**

The *Data Validation* dialog should now look like this:

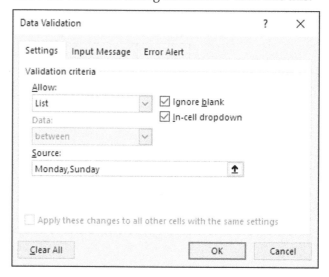

7. Click *OK*.

3 Test the new dropdown menu.

1. Click in cell D20.

A dropdown arrow should appear to the right of the cell.

2. Click the dropdown arrow and select *Sunday* from the dropdown list.

Year Planner-13

important

Magic numbers

In the spoken word it is normal to use phrases such as "the first day of the week is Monday" and "the first day of the week is Tuesday".

Functions usually prefer to work with numbers (rather than text strings) to define their arguments. In the world of programming they are often called *magic numbers*.

Later, in: *Lesson 3 6: Create formulas to determine the calendar start date*, you'll use Excel's WEEKDAY function.

The WEEKDAY function uses a magic number to determine the return value (that indicates a day of the week).

Here are the magic numbers that the WEEKDAY function recognizes:

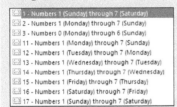

To make the *Week Start Mode* control setting "Excel Friendly" it is useful to use the same magic numbers for the control setting.

4   Create a formula in cell W4 that will return the correct *Week Start Mode* depending on whether Monday or Sunday is selected.

For the *Week Start Mode* you will use a *magic number* (see important sidebar) for the control setting rather than text.

1.   Click in cell W4.

2.   Enter the following formula:

   =IF(D20="Monday",2,1)

   This IF function simply looks for the word "Monday" in cell D20. If "Monday" is found, 2 is returned. Otherwise, 1 is returned.

5   Test the new dropdown menu again.

Use the dropdown menu in cell D20 to switch back to *Monday* as the first day of the week. When you do this, you should see the value in cell W4 change to 2.

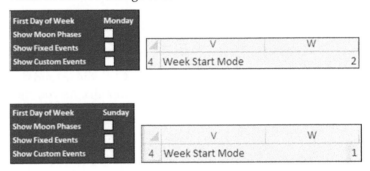

6   Save the workbook as *Year Planner-14*.

Lesson 3-4: Set control cell links

1   Open *Year Planner-14* (if it isn't already open).

2   Select the *Calendar* worksheet if it isn't already selected.

3   Set a cell link for the month selector spin button control.

     1.   Right-click the spin button control next to the month and click *Format Control* from the shortcut menu.

        The *Format Control* dialog appears.

     2.   Click the *Control* tab if it isn't already selected.

     3.   Set the *Current value* to: **1**

     4.   Set the *Minimum value* to: **1**

     5.   Set the *Maximum value* to: **12**

     6.   Set the *Cell link* to: **CalendarMonth**

        CalendarMonth is the range name that you created in: *Lesson 3-2: Define range names for the calendar control settings.*

     7.   Click *OK*.

4   Click away from the spin button control to de-select it.

5   Test the month selector spin button.

     1.   Click the up and down arrows on the spin button to switch months. As you click, you'll notice the value of cell W3 cycling from 1 to 12.

     2.   Use the spin button to change the month value to 1. This represents January.

6   Set a cell link for the year selector spin button.

     1.   Right-click the spin button next to the year.

     2.   Click *Format Control* from the shortcut menu.

        The *Format Control* dialog appears.

     3.   Click the *Control* tab if it isn't already selected.

     4.   Set the *Current value* to: **2016**

     5.   Set the *Minimum value* to: **1900**

     6.   Set the *Maximum value* to: **9999**

     7.   Set the *Cell link* to: **CalendarYear**

     8.   Click *OK*.

7   Click away from the spin button control to de-select it.

8   Test the year selector spin button.

     1.   Click the up and down arrows on the spin button to switch years. As you click, you'll notice the value of cell W2 cycling through years.

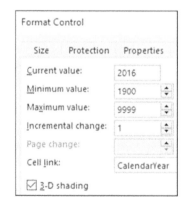

Year Planner-14

2. Use the spin button to change the year value to the year 2016.

9   Link the *Show Moon Phases* checkbox control to the *ShowMoonPhases* range name.

1. Right-click on the *Show Moon Phases* checkbox in the bottom-left corner of the calendar.

2. Click *Format Control* from the shortcut menu.

The *Format Control* dialog appears.

3. In the *Cell link* box, enter: **ShowMoonPhases**

ShowMoonPhases is the range name that you created in: *Lesson 3-2: Define range names for the calendar control settings.*

The *ShowMoonPhases* range name corresponds to cell W5.

4. Click *OK*.

10   Test the *Show Moon Phases* checkbox control.

Check and uncheck the *Show Moon Phases* checkbox. You should see the value in cell W5 change from FALSE to TRUE as you click.

11   Link the *Show Fixed Events* checkbox control to the *ShowFixedEvents* range name.

Do this in the same way as you did for the *Show Moon Phases* checkbox.

12   Link the *Show Custom Events* checkbox control to the *ShowCustomEvents* range name.

Do this in the same way as you did for the other two checkbox controls.

13   Test the three checkbox controls.

Check and uncheck each checkbox in turn.

When the checkbox is checked you should see TRUE display in the linked cell. When the checkbox is unchecked, you should see FALSE.

14   Check all three of the checkbox controls so that the moon phases and events control settings all display TRUE values.

15   Save the workbook as *Year Planner-15*.

Lesson 3-5: Create helper cells to determine the calendar start date

Using helper cells to simplify formulas

Instead of creating huge formulas that are error-prone and difficult to understand, professional Excel users break a large problem into many smaller problems using helper cells. Helper cells contain simple formulas that sequentially solve larger problems. In this lesson you'll create named helper cells to calculate the first date that needs to be displayed in the calendar.

Defining the problem

The functional specification stated:

The calendar will always show 37 days, starting with the Monday or Sunday on or before the 1st of the month that is being displayed.

Consider the test data that you manually entered:

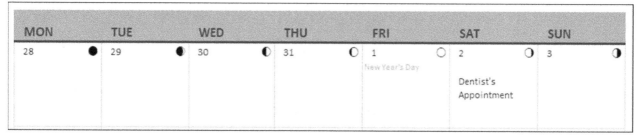

In this construction kit your first calculation task will be to calculate the first date shown in the calendar (in this example 28 December 2015). You will need to calculate this date differently depending upon whether the user has specified Sunday or Monday as the first day of the week.

This calculation is quite complicated. In this lesson you'll create helper cells to break the problem into three simpler steps:

- Calculate the *Month Start Date*.

- Use the *Month Start Date* to calculate the *Start Week Day*.

- Use the *Month Start Date* and *Start Week Day* to calculate the *Offset Start Date*.

1   Open *Year Planner-15* (if it isn't already open).

2   In cell V8, type: **Month Start Date**

3   In cell V9, type: **Start Week Day**

4   In cell V10, type: **Offset Start Date**

5   Define the range names: *MonthStartDate*, *StartWeekDay* and *OffsetStartDate* for cells W8, W9 and W10.

Year Planner-15

You learned how to do this in: *Lesson 3-2: Define range names for the calendar control settings.*

By defining names for the helper cells, you will make the formulas that reference these cells a lot more readable and less error prone.

6   Understand the purpose of each helper cell.

Week Start Mode

In the sidebar example the *Week Start Mode* contains the code number: 2. In: *Lesson 3-3: Make the first day of week selector functional,* you learned about magic numbers.

You used magic numbers to define the *Week Start Mode* as follows:

1 = Start the week on Sunday
2 = Start the week on Monday

In the test data, The *Week Start Mode* contains the number 2 indicating that the week begins on Monday.

Month Start Date

In the test data the user has selected Jan 2016 as the current month.

The starting date of Jan 2016 is, of course, 01-Jan-2016 (the first day of the selected month). The *Month Start Date* cell will contain the date serial number that represents this date (see sidebar).

Start Week Day

This cell will contain which day of the week 01-Jan-2016 fell upon expressed as a number.

01-Jan-2016 fell upon a Friday.

If the *Week Start Mode* was:

2 = Start the week on Monday

… the *Start Week Day* would need to be 5 because (starting with Monday) Friday is the fifth day of the week.

If the *Week Start Mode* was:

1 = Start the week on Sunday

… the *Start Week Day* would need to be 6 because (starting with Sunday) Friday is the sixth day of the week.

Offset Start Date

The *Offset Start Date* is the actual date that will be displayed in the first date box of the calendar. Using the test data this would need to be 28-Dec-2015 (because the test data specifies that the first day of the week is Monday and 28-Dec-2015 is the first Monday that is on or before 01-Jan-2016).

Had the first day of the week been specified as a Sunday, the *Offset Start Date* would need to be 27-Dec-2015 (because 27-Dec-2015 is the first Sunday that is on or before 01-Jan-2016).

In: *Lesson 3-6: Create formulas to determine the calendar start date,* you will add formulas to cells W8, W9 and W10 to correctly calculate these three results.

7   Save the workbook as *Year Planner-16*.

important

Date serial numbers

In Excel, every date is stored as a serial number that indicates the number of days that have elapsed since the 1st of January 1900.

The serial number for 01-Jan-2016 is 42,370 (because on 01-Jan-2016, 42,370 days had elapsed since 01-Jan-1900).

When the number 42,370 is formatted as a date (using the date format: dd-mmm-yyyy), Excel will display: 01-Jan-2016.

Because dates are stored in this way, it is very easy to add and subtract days or to find the length of time (in days) between two dates.

Many of Excel's date-related functions require a date serial number argument.

note

International date formats

Different countries use different date formats.

As this book has an international audience it is important that a date format is used that will be understandable anywhere in the world.

Month-Day-Year notation (*December 31, 2016* or *12/31/2016*) is traditionally used in the United States, but is not commonly used in other countries.

Since the 1980's the United States has been moving towards the *Day-Month-Year* notation used by most of the countries in the rest of the world.

The *Day-Month-Year* format used in the USA is generally: **31-Dec-2016**. This format is now used on US visas and passports, customs forms and for food expiration dates. It is also used for internal correspondence by the United States military.

In this book I will use the *Day-Month-Year* format (*31-Dec-2016* or *31-Dec-16*) within the text of lessons and when dates appear in the user interface.

If you prefer to use a different format in your own calendar application, everything will still work correctly.

Year Planner-16

Lesson 3-6: Create formulas to determine the calendar start date

1 Open *Year Planner-16* (if it isn't already open).

2 Create a formula in cell W8 to calculate the *Month Start Date*.

Type this date formula into cell W8:

=DATE(CalendarYear,CalendarMonth,1)

The *DATE* function accepts *Year*, *Month* and *Day* arguments and returns the *date serial number* for the appropriate date).

Notice how the named cells make the formula very easy to understand

3 Format cell W8 using the format dd-mmm-yyyy (01-Jan-2016).

1. Right-click in cell W8.

2. Click: *Format Cells* from the shortcut menu.

3. Make sure that the *Number* tab is selected and click *Custom* in the left-hand list.

4. Type: **dd-mmm-yyyy** into the *Type* box.

5. Click: OK.

4 Make the correct month and year appear in cell C11.

In cell C11, type the formula: **=MonthStartDate** and press the **<Enter>** key.

The currently selected month and year are now shown in the indigo sidebar. If you click the spin buttons you will see the month and year update to correctly represent the currently selected month and year.

5 Create a formula in cell W9 to calculate the *Start Week Day.*

In cell W9, type the following formula:

=WEEKDAY(MonthStartDate,WeekStartMode)

The WEEKDAY function accepts a *date serial number* and a *Week Start Mode* magic number that indicates the first day of the week.

You learned about magic numbers in: *Lesson 3-3: Make the first day of week selector functional.*

WeekStartMode=1: indicates that the week will run from Sunday=1 through Saturday=7.

WeekStartMode=2: indicates that the week will run from Monday=1 through Sunday=7.

The WEEKDAY function returns a number from 1 to 7, indicating the day of the week that the *Month Start Date* falls upon. In this case, the number 5 appears in cell W9, indicating that 01-Jan-2016 (a Friday) is the 5th day of the week (when the week begins on Monday).

6 Change the first day of the week to Sunday.

Use the drop-down list in cell D20 to change the starting day of the week to: *Sunday*.

Because the starting day of the week has changed, the *Week Start Mode* value in cell W4 changes from 2 to 1.

Because the *Week Start Mode* has changed, the *Start Week Day* also changes from 5 to 6. This indicates that 01-Jan-2016 (a Friday) is the 6th day of the week (when the week begins on Sunday).

7 Change the first day of the week back to Monday.

The selected first day of the week now conforms with the test data.

8 Create a formula in cell W10 to calculate the *Offset Start Date*.

The *Offset Start Date* is the first date that should appear on the calendar.

The first date to be shown on the calendar can be easily calculated using this simple formula:

=MonthStartDate-(StartWeekDay-1)

You'll remember from: *Lesson 3-5: Create helper cells to determine the calendar start date*, that Excel stores dates as date serial numbers. The date serial number defines the number of days that have elapsed since 01-Jan-1900.

For this reason, if you subtract one from 01-Jan-2016 the result will be 31-Dec-2015.

If the *Start Week Day* was 1 (meaning that the month began on a Monday) you would want the *Offset Start Date* to be the same as the *Month Start Date*. In other words, you'd want to subtract: *Start Week Day -1* (zero days) from the *Month Start Date*.

The brackets are needed to clarify precedence. Without the brackets, the formula looks like this:

=MonthStartDate-6-1 …is equivalent to: **=MonthStartDate-7**

With the brackets, the formula looks like this:

=MonthStartDate-(6-1) …is equivalent to: **=MonthStartDate-5**

The formula produces the date serial number *42366*. This is the correct result, but Excel has formatted it as an ordinary number instead of formatting it as a date.

9 Format cell W10 using the format dd-mmm-yyyy (28-Dec-2015).

10 Save the workbook as *Year Planner-17*.

Lesson 3-7: Create formulas to display each date on the calendar

Now that you know which date the calendar should start at, you can very easily create formulas to display the correct thirty-seven day numbers on the calendar.

1   Open *Year Planner-17* (if it isn't already open).

2   Create a formula to display the first date in the calendar.

   1.   In cell F4, type: **=OffsetStartDate**

   2.   Press the **<Enter>** key.

   3.   The date serial number *42366* appears.

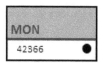

This is the correct date serial number for the 28th December 2015, but it isn't what you want to appear in the cell. All you want to see is the *Day* part of the date.

3   Format cell F4 to display the Day part of the date.

   1.   Right click cell F4 and click *Format Cells…* from the shortcut menu.

   2.   Click the *Number* tab if it isn't already selected.

   3.   Click the *Custom* option in the *Category* list.

   4.   In the *Type* box, enter: **d**

   5.   Click *OK*.

Year Planner-17

The number *28* now appears in the cell, correctly indicating 28-Dec-2015.

4   Create formulas to display all other dates in the calendar.

1. In cell H4, type: **=F4+1** and then press the **<Enter>** key.

   This simply adds one day to the date in cell F4. The formula works because the date is actually a date serial number,

2. In cell J4, type: **=H4+1** and then press the **<Enter>** key.

   Again, you're adding 1 day to the previous date. You're going to do this for every date cell in the calendar.

3. Add formulas to cells L4, N4, P4 and R4 that work in the same way, each adding 1 day to the previous date.

4. In cell F7, type: **=R4+1** and then press the **<Enter>** key.

   Again, you're simply adding 1 day to the previous date. The only difference is that the date is at the end of the calendar row above.

5. Add formulas to all of the date fields, each adding 1 day to the previous date.

5   Show gridlines and test the formulas by changing the month.

All of the formulas are now in place, but nothing appears to have changed as you're still displaying the dates for January 2016. You can easily test that the formulas are working (and are in the right cells) by enabling gridlines and changing the month that should be displayed.

1. Click: View→Show→Gridlines.

2. Use the spin buttons to change the month to Jun-2016.

3. The calendar changes to display the dates for Jun-2016.

   Confirm that you have entered the formulas correctly by comparing your calendar with the one shown below:

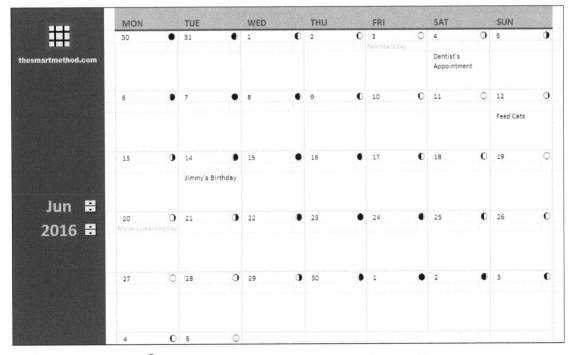

6   Save the workbook as *Year Planner-18.*

Lesson 3-8: Create formulas to display the days of the week

The calendar is now displaying the correct dates, but the days of the week shown along the top of the calendar need to be formula-driven as well.

This is because the design calls for the ability to switch between using Monday or Sunday as the first day of the Week.

1 Open *Year Planner-18* (if it isn't already open).

2 Display dates for January 2016.

Use the spin buttons to change the month and year to Jan 2016.

3 Switch to Sunday as the first day of the week.

Click in cell D20 and click *Sunday* from the drop-down list.

The calendar dates change to reflect Sunday as the first day of the week, but the days of the week in row 3 don't change.

MON	TUE	WED	THU	FRI	SAT	SUN
27	● 28	● 29	◑ 30	◑ 31	○ 1	◔ 2	◑

Year Planner-18

If you check this against another calendar, you'll see that the 27-Dec-2015 is a Sunday. Your date formulas have extracted the correct day numbers, but the days of the week labels shown above need to change.

4 Create formulas to display the correct days of the week.

1. In cell F3, type: **=F4** and then press the **<Enter>** key.

All this will do is copy the value from the cell below.

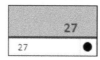

Remember that this isn't just the number 27 but is a date serial number that corresponds to 27-Dec-2015. This date serial number is currently formatted to only show the *Day* part of the date.

All of the date information is contained within the date serial number. All that you need to do is format it to display the part you need (the day of the week in textual form).

2. Change the formula to:

=TEXT(F4,"ddd")

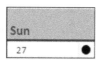

The TEXT function allows you to convert numbers and dates into text, using a custom format string such as the one you used to display the dates in: *Lesson 3-7: Create formulas to display each date on the calendar*.

This is almost what you need, but to match the design the days need to appear in upper case.

3. Change the formula to:

    =UPPER(TEXT(F4,"ddd"))

    This is exactly what you need. The correct day of the week is shown, with the correct capitalization.

4. Copy and paste the formula into cells H3, J3, L3, N3, P3 and R3.

    You can also do this by AutoFilling across, as you did in: *Lesson 2-6: Add test values*.

    The correct days of the week are now displayed:

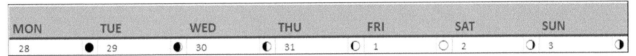

5   Test your formulas by switching to Monday as the first day of the week.

     Click in cell D20 and select *Monday* from the drop-down list.

     The dates and days of the week all change to the correct values:

MON	TUE	WED	THU	FRI	SAT	SUN
28	29	30	31	1	2	3

6   Save the workbook as *Year Planner-19*.

Lesson 3-9: Add conditional formatting to the day numbers

1   Open *Year Planner-19* (if it isn't already open).

2   Add a conditional format to the day numbers on the calendar that will make them gray if they are not within the current month.

If you refer to the design concept, you'll see that the days that are not in the currently selected month should be shown in gray. You can achieve this with a conditional format.

1. Select all of the cells that contain the day numbers on the calendar.

    These are cells F4:S4, F7:S7, F10:S10, F13:S13, F16:S16 and F19:I19.

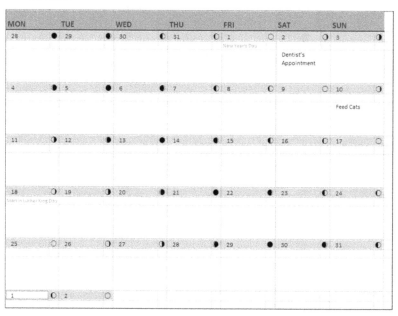

This does include the cells that contain the moon phases, but they won't be affected by the conditional format that you're going to add.

2. Click: Home→Styles→Conditional Formatting→New Rule.

3. Click *Use a formula to determine which cells to format*.

4. Enter the following formula in the *Format values where this formula is true* box:

    =MONTH(F4)<>CalendarMonth

    This formula compares the month that corresponds to the date displayed in cell F4 with the currently selected month (defined in the *CalendarMonth* range name).

    < > means 'does not equal'. This means the conditional format will format the cell if the month shown in the cell does not equal the currently selected calendar month.

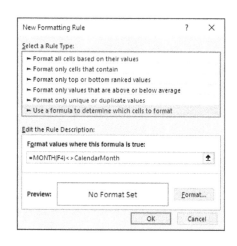

Year Planner-19

Conditional formats automatically adjust in the same way that formulas do. This means that the cell references will automatically change to correctly format each of the selected cells.

5. Click the *Format* button.

6. Click the *Font* tab.

7. Set the *Color* to *White, Background 1, Darker 25%*.

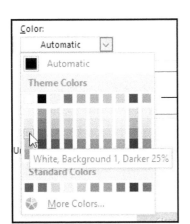

8. Click *OK* twice to close both dialogs and apply the conditional format.

   Unfortunately, this doesn't quite work properly (unless this bug has been fixed by the time you read this book) and either makes every date gray or fails to color the correct cells.

   This happened because Excel tried to automatically adjust your formula for you and made a mess of it! The work-around is to use the *Conditional Formatting Rules Manager* to correct Excel's mistake.

9. Click: Home→Styles→Conditional Formatting→ Manage Rules.

   The *Conditional Formatting Rules Manager* dialog appears, showing your conditional formatting rule.

   If your rule isn't visible, click the *Show formatting rules for* dropdown menu and select *This Worksheet*.

10. Click the *Edit Rule* button.

    You can now see why the conditional format isn't working correctly. For some reason, Excel has changed your formula from cell F4 to cell F1048565.

    Fortunately, this is easily fixed.

11. Change the formula back to: **=MONTH(F4)<>CalendarMonth**

12. Click *OK* twice to close the dialogs.

    The conditional format is now working perfectly. All of the dates that are outside the current month are shown in gray.

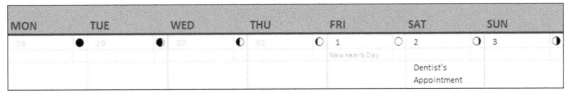

3   Save the workbook as *Year Planner-20*.

Lesson 3-10: Add conditional formatting for weekends

If you refer to the design concept, you'll see that the Saturdays and Sundays in the calendar should be shaded in a light orange color.

Because it's possible to change between using Sunday and Monday as the first day of the week, the Saturdays and Sundays are not always in the same place. The solution is to add a conditional format.

1   Open *Year Planner-20* (if it isn't already open).

2   Add a conditional format that will apply a fill color to all Saturdays and Sundays.

    1.   Select all of the cells that contain calendar days.

       These are cells F4:S18 and F19:I24.

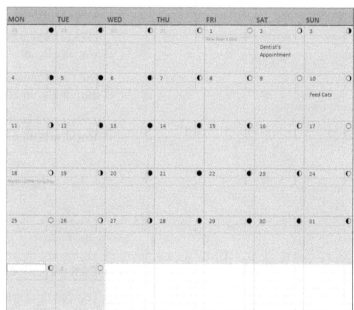

note

OR and other logical functions

The OR function checks whether any one of several conditions is true.

You're using it in this lesson to check whether the day is Saturday OR the day is Sunday.

Excel also includes several other logical functions.

The AND function checks whether all of several conditions are true.

The NOT function checks whether a condition is not true.

The XOR function is the 'exclusive or' function. It checks whether only one of several conditions is true.

Year Planner-20

       You will need to hold down the **<Ctrl>** key on your keyboard while selecting the cells in order to select this non-contiguous range.

    2.   Click: Home→Styles→Conditional Formatting→New Rule...

    3.   Click: *Use a formula to determine which cells to format*.

    4.   Enter the following formula in the *Format values where this formula is true* box:

       =OR(F$3="SAT",F$3="SUN")

       The OR function allows you to check for more than one condition. This formula will check whether the value in cell F3 is either SAT or SUN.

       Notice that you're using the mixed reference F$3 instead of simply referring to cell F3. This will allow the conditional format to adjust the column part of the reference, but not the row part.

This means that in cell H7, the formula will automatically adjust to check cell H3 for the day of the week. F is allowed to change to H, but 3 has to stay the same so that it is always referencing the days of the week in row 3.

5. Click the *Format* button.

6. Click the *Fill* tab and set the *Background Color* to *Orange, Accent 2, Lighter 80%* (the lightest orange color).

7. Click *OK* twice to close the dialogs.

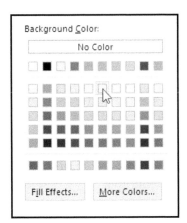

The conditional format is applied, but there's a small problem. It is working perfectly for the days and events, but the cells containing the moon phases aren't being shaded.

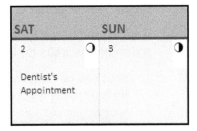

This problem has been caused by the way that Excel automatically adjusts the formulas used by conditional formatting rules.

In cells P4, P5 and P6 the conditional format looks for SAT or SUN in cell P3, which is correct. However, in cells Q4 and Q5 the conditional format is referencing cell Q3. Cell Q3 is empty, so the conditional format can't tell that this is a Saturday.

This could be solved by making the formula more complicated, but a simpler solution is to add a second conditional format to cater for the moon phases. You'll do this in the next lesson.

3   Save the workbook as *Year Planner-21*.

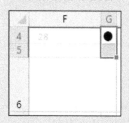
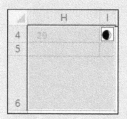
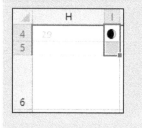
Lesson 3-11: Add conditional formatting for the moon phases

In the previous lesson you created a conditional format to shade all Saturday and Sunday cells, but it wasn't possible to shade the moon phases with a single conditional format.

You'll add a second conditional format in this lesson that will shade the moon phase cells.

1 Open *Year Planner-21* (if it isn't already open).

2 Add a conditional format that will apply a fill color to the moon phase cells on Saturdays and Sundays.

1. Select all of the cells containing moon phases, making sure to include the empty cell below each moon phase.

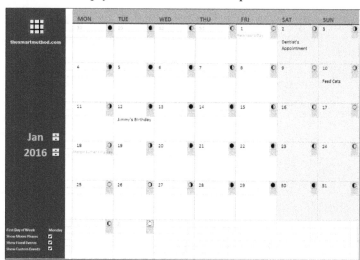

Remember that you will need to hold down the **<Ctrl>** key while selecting the cells. Excel 2019 also allows you to deselect cells if you make a mistake (see sidebar).

2. Click: Home→Styles→Conditional Formatting→New Rule.

3. Create another conditional format with exactly the same settings as the one you created in: *Lesson 3-10: Add conditional formatting for weekends.*

Use this formula (the same formula you used last time)

=OR(F$3="SAT",F$3="SUN")

You need to also apply the same light orange shading.

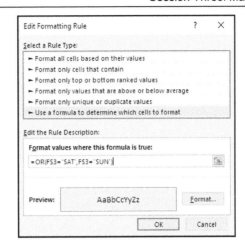

4. Click *OK* to apply the new conditional format.

   Unfortunately, Excel will try to help by auto-adjusting your formula again (from F$3 to D$3), resulting in a conditional format that doesn't work.

5. Open the *Conditional Formatting Rules Manager* and edit the new rule back to the correct formula of:

   =OR(F$3="SAT",F$3="SUN")

   Do this in the same way as you did in: *Lesson 3-10: Add conditional formatting for weekends.*

6. Click *OK* to apply the modified conditional format.

3 Test the conditional formats by switching between Sunday and Monday as the first day of the week.

Do this by using the dropdown menu in cell D20.

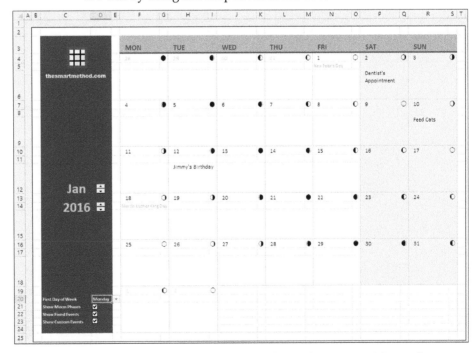

The shaded columns move to indicate the new positions of Saturday and Sunday. Your conditional formats are now complete.

4 Save the workbook as *Year Planner-22*.

Session Four: Implement fixed events

> Events will take their course, it is no good of being angry at them; he is happiest who wisely turns them to the best account.
>
> *Euripides, Greek poet (484 BC - 406 BC).*

In this session, you'll add fixed events to the calendar.

All of the events that are defined in the functional specification except Easter Sunday are logically defined by referencing dates. This means that the date they fall upon in any future year can be precisely calculated using Excel functions and formulas.

Easter Sunday is an exception. It is extremely difficult to use logic to predict which day Easter Sunday will fall upon in the coming years as the dates are defined based upon the phases of the moon

In this lesson you'll learn techniques that will enable you to define the US national holidays listed in the objectives below. The skills you'll learn will also empower you to calculate the future date of any fixed event that is logically defined.

You'll also learn a different technique to determine the future dates of Easter Sunday (and any other future event that is not logically defined).

Session Objectives

By the end of this session you will have:

- Created a table for fixed events
- Linked the table of fixed events to the calendar
- Added fixed-date national holidays
- Found the first named day in a month
- Calculated dates for common US public holidays
- Found the last named day in a month
- Calculated the date for Memorial Day
- Calculated the date for Easter Sunday
- Connected Public Holidays to the FixedEvents table

Lesson 4-1: Create a table for fixed events

Before you can begin defining your fixed events, you will need to create a table to store them. This will be hidden from the user in the final version of the year planner.

1   Open *Year Planner-22* (if it isn't already open).

2   Create a new worksheet, named: **Fixed Events**

    1.   Click the *New sheet* icon below the worksheet: ⊕

        A new worksheet appears.

    2.   Right click the new worksheet's tab and click *Rename* from the shortcut menu.

    3.   Type **Fixed Events** and press the **<Enter>** key.

3   In cell A1, type: **Fixed Events** and press the **<Enter>** key.

4   Apply the *Title* style to cell A1.

    1.   Select cell A1.

    2.   Click: Home→Styles→Cell Styles Gallery→Title.

5   Enter data for custom events.

Enter the following data into cells A3:B4, resizing the columns as needed:

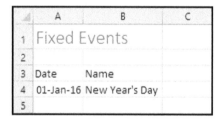

6   Define the fixed events data as a Table.

    1.   Select cells A3:B4.

    2.   Click: Insert→Tables→Table.

    3.   Click *OK* when prompted.

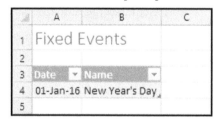

The colors change and filter arrows appear, indicating that a Table has been defined. You will define the fixed events that should appear in the calendar in this table.

Because fixed events will be defined in a Table, the calendar's formulas will continue to work correctly if rows are added or removed.

Year Planner-22

7 Set the name of the Table to: **FixedEvents**

1. Click anywhere in the Table.

2. Click: Table Tools→Design→Properties→Table Name.

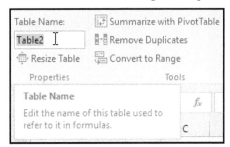

3. Type: **FixedEvents** and press the **<Enter>** key.

You've now named your table so that it can be easily accessed by the formulas that you will add to the calendar later.

8 Create a formula for New Year's Day in cell A4.

You've entered the 1st of January 2016 into cell A4. This is the correct date for New Year's Day, but it will only be correct if the calendar is set to display the year 2016.

To work correctly, this date needs to automatically adjust to show New Year's Day for the selected year.

Enter the following formula in cell A4 to calculate the date of New Year's Day:

=DATE(CalendarYear,1,1)

This DATE function simply returns 01-Jan for whichever year is currently selected in the calendar. As you currently have 2016 selected, 01-Jan-16 is returned.

9 Save the workbook as *Year Planner-23*.

note

Alternatives to VLOOKUP

VLOOKUP is the correct choice in almost every case where you need to search for a value within a table and return a corresponding value.

Excel also offers the HLOOKUP function for tables that run across several columns instead of down several rows.

It's possible to get the same results as VLOOKUP by using the MATCH and INDEX functions, but this will result in a more complex formula.

MATCH and INDEX can be useful in rare cases when you need to look up values in an unusual way, but VLOOKUP offers the best solution in most situations.

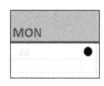

Year Planner-23

Lesson 4-2: Link the table of fixed events to the calendar

In this lesson, you'll link your table of fixed events to the calendar so that the fixed events are displayed on the correct dates. This will allow you to test that your fixed events are working correctly.

1   Open *Year Planner-23* (if it isn't already open).

2   Select the *Calendar* worksheet if it isn't already selected.

3   Make sure that all three check boxes are checked.

4   Make sure the First Day of Week is set to Monday.

5   Select *Jan 2016* using the spin button controls.

6   Add a VLOOKUP formula to cell F5 that will retrieve any fixed events for the date in cell F4.

   1.   Enter the following formula into cell F5:

        =VLOOKUP(F4,FixedEvents,2,FALSE)

   2.   Press the **<Enter>** key.

        An error message is displayed:

The VLOOKUP function searches a range of data for a value and returns a corresponding result. In this case you're searching for the date within the *FixedEvents* table, and returning the value found in column 2: the name of the event.

An error has been returned because the VLOOKUP function couldn't find any events for 28-Dec-15. When a VLOOKUP function can't find a match, it returns an error.

You don't want these errors to appear, so you'll need to revise the formula.

7   Revise the formula to suppress error messages.

   1.   Revise the formula in cell F5 to:

        =IFERROR(VLOOKUP(F4,FixedEvents,2,FALSE),"")

   2.   Press the **<Enter>** key.

        The IFERROR function allows you to choose what is shown if an error occurs. In this case, you're using an empty set of quote marks to indicate that nothing should be shown if there is an error (meaning that no fixed event has been defined for this day).

        This time, the formula works correctly and nothing is shown in cell H5.

8   Revise the formula to respect the *Show Fixed Events* setting.

You'll remember that the user needs to be able to show and hide the fixed events by using the checkbox in the bottom left corner. To make this possible, you'll need to revise the formula one more time.

Revise the formula to:

**=IF(ShowFixedEvents=TRUE,
IFERROR(VLOOKUP(F4,FixedEvents,2,FALSE),""),"")**

The additional IF function checks whether the value in the *ShowFixedEvents* range name is TRUE or FALSE. If it's FALSE, it returns a blank cell.

You created the *ShowFixedEvents* range name in: *Lesson 3-2: Define range names for the calendar control settings.*

9   Fill the formula across to column S.

1.   Select cells F5:G5.

2.   Click and drag the fill handle to the right, all the way to cell S5.

Notice that (provided that Jan 2016 is still selected as the current month) New Year's Day is shown on 1ˢᵗ January. Try changing the *First Day of Week* from Monday to Sunday and back. Notice that New Year's Day is always shown in the correct box.

10   Copy the formulas from row 5 to the other fixed events rows.

1.   Select cells F5:S5.

2.   Copy the selected cells by pressing **<Ctrl>+<C>** or clicking: Home→Clipboard→Copy.

3.   Paste into cells F8, F11, F14 and F17.

4.   Copy cells F5:I5.

5.   Paste into cell F20.

All of the formulas are now in place to display any fixed events that are listed in the *FixedEvents* table in the *Fixed Events* worksheet.

11   Test that fixed events are displaying correctly and that the Show Fixed Events checkbox can be used to remove them.

1.   Use the calendar controls to select January 2017.

2.   If the formula is working correctly, *New Year's Day* should appear beneath 01-Jan.

3.   Uncheck the *Show Fixed Events* checkbox.

New Year's Day should disappear from the 01-Jan box.

4.   Check all three checkboxes.

12   Save the workbook as *Year Planner-24.*

---

note

Logical expressions can consist of a single range name or cell reference

In this lesson you use the following formula:

**=IF(ShowFixedEvents=TRUE,
IFERROR(VLOOKUP(F4,Fixe
dEvents,2,FALSE),""),"")**

The formula would still work perfectly if the logical expresson was simply:

ShowFixedEvents

… rather than:

ShowFixedEvents=TRUE

The full formula would then be:

**=IF(ShowFixedEvents,
IFERROR(VLOOKUP(F4,Fixe
dEvents,2,FALSE),""),"")**

When I am teaching I prefer to include **=TRUE** as I think it makes it easier for students to understand the formula.

You may wish to use the simpler form in your own real-world work.

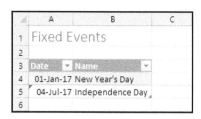

Lesson 4-3: Add fixed-date national holidays

National holidays are not all calculated in the same way, but some fall on the same date each year. These are the easiest to calculate, so you'll begin by adding the national holidays that have fixed dates.

You'll add national holidays that can have different dates each year later.

1 Open *Year Planner-24* (if it isn't already open).

2 Select the *Fixed Events* worksheet if it isn't already selected.

3 Add *Independence Day* to the Table, with a formula that will calculate the correct date for any year.

Independence Day always falls on 04-Jul each year, so the formula to calculate it is quite simple.

1. Click in cell B4 and press the **<Tab>** key.

   This will add a new row to the Table.

2. In cell A5, enter the following formula:

   =DATE(CalendarYear,7,4)

3. Press the **<Enter>** key.

   This formula simply returns the date serial number for 04-Jul for the selected year.

   It's possible that, when you enter this formula, the date for New Year's Day will also update to 04-Jul. This is because, by default, Excel's *Tables* feature tries to keep formulas consistent by automatically adjusting them.

   If this happens, you should see a Smart Tag icon appear:

   Click this icon and click *Undo Calculated Column*.

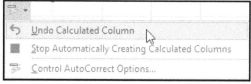

This will allow you to enter the formulas you need without permanently disabling the feature.

If you clicked *Stop Automatically Creating Calculated Columns*, you would permanently stop Excel from automatically adjusting formulas when they are entered into Tables (see sidebar).

4. In cell B5, type: **Independence Day**

4 Add *Veterans Day* to the Table, with a formula that will calculate the correct date for any year.

Veterans day always falls on 11-Nov each year.

1. Click in cell B5 and press the **<Tab>** key to add a new row to the table.

2.   In cell A6, enter the following formula:

=DATE(CalendarYear,11,11)

Just as with the other formulas, this returns 11-Nov for whichever year is selected in the calendar.

See step 2 if the date of New Year's Day changes when you enter this formula.

3.   In cell B6, enter: **Veterans Day**

5   Add *Christmas Day* to the Table, with a formula that will calculate the correct date for any year.

Christmas day always falls on 25-Dec each year.

1.   Click in cell B6 and press the **<Tab>** key to add a new row to the table.

2.   In cell A7, enter the following formula:

=DATE(CalendarYear,12,25)

3.   In cell B7, enter: **Christmas Day**

6   Check that the holidays are being displayed correctly in the calendar.

1.   Click the *Calendar* worksheet tab.

2.   Use the calendar controls to set the month to Jul-2017.

3.   Confirm that Independence Day appears on 04-Jul.

4.   Set the month to Nov-2017 and confirm that Veterans Day appears on 11-Nov.

5.   Switch to Dec-2017 and confirm that Christmas Day appears on 25-Dec.

6.   Switch to Dec-2016 and confirm that Christmas Day is still appearing, even though the year has changed.

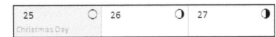

7.   Check and uncheck the *Show Fixed Events* checkbox and confirm that fixed events do not display when the checkbox is not checked.

8.   Check all three checkboxes.

9.   Return the selected month to Jan-2016.

7   Save the workbook as *Year Planner-25*.

Lesson 4-4: Find the first named day in a month

Some U.S. public holidays fall on different dates each year. Here is how they are defined:

Holiday	Date
Martin Luther King Day	The third Monday in January
President's Day	The third Monday in February
Labor Day	The first Monday in September
Columbus Day	The second Monday in October
Thanksgiving Day	The fourth Thursday in November

It can be seen that a common format for a public holiday is:

The [Nth] [Day Name] in [Month Name]

Catering for future expansion with a generic solution

Even though the functional specification doesn't demand it, you will implement a solution that can be applied to any date that is defined in the above way.

The generic solution will make it easy to add other events to the calendar such as: *The second Wednesday in March* with very little effort. This will also make it easier for students in other countries to simply replace U.S. public holidays with their own.

Why this problem is difficult to solve

Finding dates such as *the third Monday in January* is very simple for humans to understand but is a little more challenging for Excel. The problem arises because months have a variable number of days and can begin on a different day each year.

In this lesson you'll use a novel (and simple) technique using a lookup table.

1   Open *Year Planner-25* (if it isn't already open).

2   Add a new worksheet and name it: **Public Holidays**

3   Click in cell A1 of the new worksheet and type: **Public Holidays** (followed by the **<Enter>** key).

4   Apply the *Title* style to cell A1.

   1.   Click in cell A1 to select it.

   2.   Click: Home→Styles→Cell Styles→Title.

5   Add the data shown below to cells A3:F10.

Year Planner-25

	A	B	C	D	E	F
3	First Day of Month	First Mon	First Tue	First Wed	First Thu	First Fri
4	Tue	7	1	2	3	4
5	Wed	6	7	1	2	3
6	Thu	5	6	7	1	2
7	Fri	4	5	6	7	1
8	Sat	3	4	5	6	7
9	Sun	2	3	4	5	6
10	Mon	1	2	3	4	5

The above data defines the first occurrence of a specific day (for example *Thu*) in a month when the name of the first day of the month is known.

For example, if the first day of a month was *Thursday*, the first *Tuesday* of that month would occur on 6th day of the month (shown shaded in the above screen grab).

6   Convert the range: A3:F7 into a Table named: **FirstDay**

1.   Click anywhere inside the range.

2.   Click: Insert→Tables→Table and then click: OK.

3.   Click: Table Tools→Design→Properties→Table Name.

4.   Type: **FirstDay** and press the **<Enter>** key.

5.   Click: Data→Sort & Filter→Filter.

This will remove the drop-down filter arrows.

7   Define public holidays in an Excel-friendly format.

While it is normal to use names such as *January* and *February* in the spoken word, Excel prefers to work with numbers (such as 1 and 2).

Enter the following data in cells A12:F15 to define five public holidays in an Excel-friendly format.

	A	B	C	D	E	F
12	Holiday	MLK	Presidents	Labor	Columbus	Thanksgiving
13	Month (1=Jan, 12=Dec)	1	2	9	10	11
14	Day (1=Mon, 7=Sun)	1	1	1	1	4
15	Offset (Days after first ocurrence)	14	14	0	7	21

(In the above screen grab the *Heading 3* style has been applied to cells A12:F12. You learned how to apply styles in: *Lesson 2-12: Create a table for non-recurring custom events*).

Consider *Thanksgiving Day*.

•   You can see that it occurs in month 11. The eleventh month of the year is November.

•   You can see that it occurs on day 4 of the week. Day 4 is a Thursday.

•   You can see that it is offset by 21 days from the first Thursday in the month of November.

This is an Excel-friendly way of defining that Thanksgiving Day occurs on the third Thursday in November.

8   Save the workbook as *Year Planner-26*.

note

An alternative method

It is possible to calculate *Martin Luther King Day* (the third Monday in January) by combining DATE, WEEKDAY and MOD functions.

If the 1st of January fell on a Monday, the third Monday would be on the 15th of January. This means that the 15th of January is the *earliest* possible date that Martin Luther King Day could occur.

This can be easily calculated like this:

=DATE(CalendarYear, 1, 15)

The WEEKDAY and MOD function can then be used to extend the formula as follows:

=DATE(CalendarYear,1,15)+ MOD(7-WEEKDAY(DATE(CalendarYear,1,15),3),7)

Here's how the formula works:

WEEKDAY(DATE(CalendarYear,1,15),3)

…calculates the day of the week for the 15th of January. The code number 3 indicates that the function should return Mon=0 through to Sun=6.

This means you can calculate the correct date by adding 7 to the 15th of January, minus the result of the WEEKDAY function.

For example, if 15-Jan is a Tuesday, the full formula will return 21-Jan, as the formula works like this:

=15-Jan + (7 – 1) = 21-Jan

The MOD function is needed to cater for the exception when 15-Jan is already a Monday. The MOD function works because Monday alone will return zero when divided by seven.

Year Planner-26

Lesson 4-5: Calculate dates for common US public holidays

In: *Lesson 4-4: Find the first named day in a month,* you created a lookup table to quickly determine the day of any month in which a specific day first occurred (when the weekday name of the first day in the month is known).

You also defined the dates of five US public holidays in an Excel-friendly format. Here is the worksheet you created:

	A	B	C	D	E	F
1	Public Holidays					
2						
3	First Day Of Month	First Mon	First Tue	First Wed	First Thur	First Fri
4	Tue	7	1	2	3	4
5	Wed	6	7	1	2	3
6	Thu	5	6	7	1	2
7	Fri	4	5	6	7	1
8	Sat	3	4	5	6	7
9	Sun	2	3	4	5	6
10	Mon	1	2	3	4	5
11						
12	Holiday	MLK	Presidents	Labor	Columbus	Thanksgiving
13	Month (1=Jan, 12=Dec)	1	2	9	10	11
14	Day (1=Mon, 7=Sun)	1	1	1	1	4
15	Offset (Days after first ocurrence)	14	14	0	7	21

In this lesson you will use the above public holiday definitions and lookup table to determine the precise dates for the five defined public holidays in any year. Here is the methodology you will use to calculate the correct date for Martin Luther King Day in 2017 (the third Monday in January 2017):

1. Calculate the *first date of the month* in which MLK Day falls. You can see that MLK Day is in Month 1 (January). The result of the calculation will be: **01-Jan-17**.

2. Calculate the *weekday name of the first day of the month* in which MLK Day falls. The result of the calculation will be: **Sunday** (because 01-Jan-17 falls on a Sunday)

3. Calculate the day part of the date of the *first occurrence* of **Monday** in Jan-17 (because Martin Luther King Day falls on a Monday).

   The lookup table makes this easy because you already know that the *weekday name of the first day of the month* in Jan-17 is Sunday.

   The result of the calculation will be 2 (cell B9 in the lookup table) as 02-Jan-17 is the first Monday in the month of January 2017.

4. Determine the precise date of MLK Day. To do this you need to offset the date by 14 days (two weeks). 14 days after 02-Jan-17 is 16-Jan-17. This is the correct date for MLK Day in 2017.

1   Open *Year Planner-26* (if it isn't already open) and set the calendar to display dates for any month in 2017.

2   Select the *Public Holidays* worksheet.

3   In cell A17, type: **First Date of Month**

note

Yet another alternative solution using the CHOOSE function

In the facing page's sidebar, a complex formula-based solution was described that could calculate Martin Luther King Day using a combination of DATE, WEEKDAY and MOD functions.

The MOD function was used to enable the formula to convert the possible numbers 1, 2, 3, 4, 5, 6 and 7 into 1, 2, 3, 4, 5, 6 and 0.

Some users find the MOD function difficult to understand and prefer an alternative solution using the CHOOSE function.

The CHOOSE function accepts sequential numbers and then returns any numbers that you specify.

For example:

=CHOOSE(A1,67,23,54)

…would return 67 if cell A1 contained the number 1, 23 if cell A1 contained the number 2, and 54 if cell A1 contained the number 3.

Here's how you could use the CHOOSE function instead of the MOD function:

=DATE(CalendarYear,1,15) +CHOOSE(7-WEEKDAY(DATE(CalendarYear,1,15),3), 1,2,3,4,5,6,0)

You could argue that the MOD solution, produces a more compact formula that presents fewer opportunities to enter the wrong value by mistake.

There are many other methods to calculate Martin Luther King Day, but none are as versatile and easily understood as the VLOOKUP based solution presented in this lesson.

4   Add a formula to cell B17 to calculate the first date of the month in which the Martin Luther King public holiday falls.

   1.   In cell B17, type the formula: **=DATE(CalendarYear, B13, 1)**

   2.   Press the **<Enter>** key.

   3.   The date *01-Jan-2017* appears in cell B17.

5   In cell A18, type: **First Day of Month**

6   Add a formula to cell B18 to calculate the weekday that the first day of the month falls upon.

   1.   In cell B18, type the formula: **=TEXT(B17, "ddd")**

   2.   Press the **<Enter>** key.

      The TEXT function has applied the custom format "ddd" to the date serial number in cell B17.

      The text *Sun* appears in cell B18, indicating that the first day of Jan-17 was a Sunday.

7   In cell A19, type: **First Occurrence**

8   Add a formula to cell B19 to calculate the day part of the date of the first Monday in January 2017.

   Insert a VLOOKUP function into cell B19. The correct arguments are:

   The value returned is 2. (You may have to re-format this value as a number if it is formatted as a date by default).

9   In cell A20, type: **Date**

10   Add a formula to cell B20 to calculate the correct date for MLK Day in 2017.

   1.   In cell B20, type the formula:

      =DATE(CalendarYear, B13,B19+B15)

   2.   Press the **<Enter>** key.

   3.   The date: 16-Jan-17 appears in cell B20. This is the correct date for *Martin Luther King Day* in 2017.

11   AutoFill cells B17:B20 across to cells C17:F20.

⊿	A	B	C	D	E	F
12	Holiday	MLK	Presidents	Labor	Columbus	Thanksgiving
17	First Date of Month	01-Jan-2017	01-Feb-2017	01-Sep-2017	01-Oct-2017	01-Nov-2017
18	First Day of Month	Sun	Wed	Fri	Sun	Wed
19	First Occurrence	2	6	4	2	2
20	Date	16-Jan-2017	20-Feb-2017	04-Sep-2017	09-Oct-2017	23-Nov-2017

12   Save the workbook as *Year Planner-27*.

Lesson 4-6: Find the last named day in a month

Another common format for a public holiday (or other event) is:

The [Nth] last [Day Name] in [Month Name]

Memorial Day is defined in this way and falls on the last Monday in May.

Catering for future expansion with a generic solution

Even though the functional specification doesn't demand it, you will implement a solution that can be applied to any date that is defined in the above way.

It will be easy in the future for you to add events to the calendar such as: *The last Wednesday in July* with very little effort.

Why this problem is difficult to solve

Finding dates such as *the last Monday in May* is very simple for humans to understand but is a little more challenging for Excel. The problem arises because months have a variable number of days and can end on a different day each year.

In this lesson you'll use a similar technique to that used in: *Lesson 4-4: Find the first named day in a month,* by using a lookup table.

1　Open *Year Planner-27* (if it isn't already open).

2　Select the *Public Holidays* worksheet if it isn't already selected.

3　Add the data shown below to cells A22:F29.

	A	B	C	D	E	F
22	Last Day of Month	Last Mon	Last Tue	Last Wed	Last Thu	Last Fri
23	Tue	-1	0	-6	-5	-4
24	Wed	-2	-1	0	-6	-5
25	Thu	-3	-2	-1	0	-6
26	Fri	-4	-3	-2	-1	0
27	Sat	-5	-4	-3	-2	-1
28	Sun	-6	-5	-4	-3	-2
29	Mon	0	-6	-5	-4	-3

The above data defines the last occurrence of a specific day (for example *Thu*) in a month when the name of the last day of the month is known.

For example: If the last day of a month was *Thursday*, the last *Tuesday* of that month would occur two days before the last day of the month (shown shaded in the above screen grab).

4　Convert the range: A3:F7 into a Table named: **LastDay**

1. Click anywhere inside the range.

2. Click: Insert→Tables→Table.

3. Click: OK.

Year Planner-27

4.   Click: Table Tools→Design→Properties→Table Name.

5.   Type: **LastDay**

6.   Press the **<Enter>** key.

7.   Click: Data→Sort & Filter→Filter.

This will remove the drop-down filter arrows.

5   Define *Memorial Day* in an Excel-friendly format.

While it is normal to use names such as *January* and *February* in the spoken word, Excel prefers to work with numbers (such as 1 and 2).

Enter the following data in cells A31:B34 to define *Memorial Day* in an Excel-friendly format.

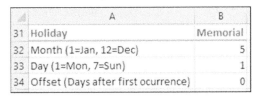

(In the above screen grab the *Heading 3* style has been applied to cells A12:F12. You learned how to apply styles in: *Lesson 2-12: Create a table for non-recurring custom events*).

•   You can see that Memorial Day occurs in *Month 5* (May).

•   You can see that Memorial Day occurs on *Day 1* of the week (Mon).

•   You can see that Memorial Day is offset by zero days from the last Monday in the month of May.

This is a long-winded way of saying that Memorial Day occurs on the last Monday in May.

This setting isn't needed for Memorial Day but will enable you to simply specify dates such as: *the second to last Friday in June* should you need to add them in the future.

6   Save the workbook as *Year Planner-28*.

note

An alternative method

It is possible to calculate *Memorial Day* (the last Monday in May) by combining WEEKDAY and DATE functions like this:

=DATE(CalendarYear,5,31)-WEEKDAY(DATE(CalendarYear,5,31),3)

Here's how the formula works:

=DATE(CalendarYear,5,31)

Instead of starting with the earliest possible date for Memorial Day, the formula begins by calculating the latest.

31-May is the latest possible date upon which Memorial Day could occur.

If 31-May is a Monday, it will be Memorial Day.

-WEEKDAY(DATE(CalendarYear,5,31),3)

In: *Lesson 3-3: Make the first day of week selector functional,* you learned that the WEEKDAY function uses the following *magic numbers* to determine the return value:

1 - Numbers 1 (Sunday) through 7 (Saturday)
2 - Numbers 1 (Monday) through 7 (Sunday)
3 - Numbers 0 (Monday) through 6 (Sunday)
11 - Numbers 1 (Monday) through 7 (Sunday)
12 - Numbers 1 (Tuesday) through 7 (Monday)
13 - Numbers 1 (Wednesday) through 7 (Tuesday)
14 - Numbers 1 (Thursday) through 7 (Wednesday)
15 - Numbers 1 (Friday) through 7 (Thursday)
16 - Numbers 1 (Saturday) through 7 (Friday)
17 - Numbers 1 (Sunday) through 7 (Saturday)

Because the formula uses the magic number 3 as the second argument of the WEEKDAY function, 0-6 is returned indicating Monday-Sunday.

This means you can simply subtract the result of the WEEKDAY function from the 31st of May to calculate the correct date for Memorial Day.

Lesson 4-7: Calculate the date for Memorial Day

Memorial Day falls on the last Monday in May.

In: *Lesson 4-6: Find the last named day in a* month, you created a lookup table to quickly determine the day in any month in which a specific day last occurred (provided that you know the weekday name of the last day in the month).

You also defined the date that *Memorial Day* falls on in an Excel-friendly format. Here is the worksheet you created:

	A	B	C	D	E	F
22	**Last Day Of Month**	**Last Mon**	**Last Tue**	**Last Wed**	**Last Thur**	**Last Fri**
23	Tue	-1	0	-6	-5	-4
24	Wed	-2	-1	0	-6	-5
25	Thu	-3	-2	-1	0	-6
26	Fri	-4	-3	-2	-1	0
27	Sat	-5	-4	-3	-2	-1
28	Sun	-6	-5	-4	-3	-2
29	Mon	0	-6	-5	-4	-3
30						
31	Holiday	Memorial				
32	Month (1=Jan, 12=Dec)	5				
33	Day (1=Mon, 7=Sun)	1				
34	Offset (Days before first ocurrence)	0				

In this lesson you will use the above Memorial Day definition and *LastDay* lookup table to determine the precise date that Memorial Day falls upon in any year.

Here is the methodology you will use to calculate the correct date for Memorial Day in 2017:

1. Calculate the *last date of the month* in which Memorial Day falls. You can see that Memorial Day is in Month 5 (May). The result of the calculation will be: **31-May-17**.

2. Calculate the *weekday name of the last day of the month* in which Memorial Day falls. The result of the calculation will be: **Wednesday**.

3. Calculate the date of the *last occurrence* of Monday in May 2017.

   The lookup table makes this easy because you already know that the *Last Day of Month* to lookup is Wednesday.

   The result of the calculation will be -2, as the last Monday in May 2017 falls two days before the last day of the month (which is Wednesday).

4. Determine the precise date of Memorial Day. If you move backwards two days before 31-May the result is 29-May. This was the correct date for Memorial Day in 2017. In the case of Memorial Day no offset is needed. In this generic solution, the offset is provided to enable you to define a date such as "the second to last Tuesday in June" (when the offset would be -7).

1 Open *Year Planner-28* (if it isn't already open).

2 Select the *Public Holidays* worksheet if it isn't already selected.

3   In cell A36, type: **Last Date of Month**

4   Add a formula to cell B36 to calculate the last date of the month in which the Memorial Day public holiday falls.

  1. In cell B36, type the formula:

      =DATE(CalendarYear, B32+1,1)-1

  2. Press the **<Enter>** key.

      The date *31-May-2017* appears in cell B36

5   In cell A37, type: **Last Day of Month**

6   Add a formula to cell B37 to calculate the weekday that the last day of the month falls upon.

  1. In cell B37, type the formula: **=TEXT(B36, "ddd")**

  2. Press the **<Enter>** key.

      The TEXT function has applied the custom format "ddd" to the date serial number in cell B36. The text *Wed* appears in cell B37 indicating that the last day of May 2017 was a Wednesday.

7   In cell A38, type: **Offset**

8   Add a formula to cell B38 to calculate the day part of the date of the last Monday in May 2017.

    Insert a VLOOKUP function into cell B38. The correct arguments are:

    The value returned is -2. (You may have to re-format this value as a number if it is formatted as a date by default).

9   In cell A39, type: **Date**

10   Add a formula to cell B39 to calculate the correct date for Memorial Day in 2017.

  1. In cell B39, type the formula:

      =B36+B38-B34

  2. Press the **<Enter>** key.

      The date: 29-May-2017 appears in cell B39. This is the correct date for *Memorial Day* in 2017.

31	Holiday	Memorial
32	Month (1=Jan, 12=Dec)	5
33	Day (1=Mon, 7=Sun)	1
34	Offset (Days after first ocurrence)	0
35		
36	Last Date of Month	31-May-2017
37	Last Day of Month	Wed
38	Offset	-2
39	Date	29-May-2017

11   Save the workbook as *Year Planner-29*.

Year Planner-29

Lesson 4-8: Calculate the date for Easter Sunday

Easter Sunday is much more difficult to calculate than any of the other national holidays. Instead of being determined by days of the week, Easter Sunday is defined based upon the spring equinox and phases of the moon.

Easter Sunday falls upon the *first Sunday after the first full moon following the spring equinox.* You're going to add formulas to calculate the phases of the moon later in this construction kit, but even though they will reasonably accurately predict the phase of the moon (within around plus or minus seven hours), they won't be accurate enough to reliably predict the precise date of Easter Sunday.

To predict the date of Easter Sunday with complete certainty, you would need some extremely complex formulas. Since the functional specification only calls for the calendar to work for dates from 100 years in the past to 100 years in the future, a better solution is simply to pre-calculate the dates for all of the Easter Sundays within those 200 years.

1 Open *Year Planner-29* (if it isn't already open).

2 Open *EasterDates* from your sample files folder.

This workbook contains the dates for every Easter Sunday from 1901 to 2115, contained in a table named *EasterDates*.

3 Select columns A and B and copy them.

4 Return to the *Year Planner-29* workbook.

5 Select the *Fixed Events* worksheet.

6 Paste the Easter dates into cell D1.

	A	B	C	D	E
1	Fixed Events			Easter Dates	
2					
3	Date	Name		Year	Date
4	01-Jan-17	New Year's Day		1901	07-Apr-1901
5	04-Jul-17	Independence Day		1902	30-Mar-1902
6	11-Nov-17	Veterans Day		1903	12-Apr-1903
7	25-Dec-17	Christmas Day		1904	03-Apr-1904
8				1905	23-Apr-1905
9				1906	15-Apr-1906

The *EasterDates* table has now been added to the *FixedEvents* worksheet.

7 Add Easter Sunday to the FixedEvents table, with a formula that will return the correct date for any year between 1901 and 2115.

1. Click in cell B7 and press the **<Tab>** key.

This will add a new row to the Table.

2. Add the following formula in cell A8:

=VLOOKUP(CalendarYear,EasterDates,2,FALSE)

This VLOOKUP formula simply searches through the *EasterDates* table, searching for the currently selected year.

3. In cell B9, type: **Easter Sunday**

8 Check that the formula is working correctly on the calendar.

1. Click the *Calendar* worksheet tab.

2. Use the calendar controls to switch to April 2017.

Easter Sunday should appear on the 16th of April.

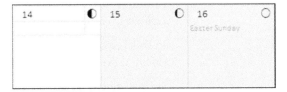

9 Save the workbook as *Year Planner-30*.

Lesson 4-9: Connect Public Holidays to the FixedEvents table

The calendar automatically populates dates defined in the *FixedEvents* table (located on the Fixed Events worksheet).

Public Holidays are currently defined in different cells within the *Public Holidays* worksheet.

In this lesson you will add Public Holidays to the the *FixedEvents* table (located on the Fixed Events worksheet).

To avoid errors this will be done using single-cell range names.

1　Open *Year Planner-30* (if it isn't already open).

2　Select the *Public Holidays* worksheet (if it isn't already selected).

3　Click on cell B20 (the cell containing the calculated date of Martin Luther King Day).

4　Define a range name for this cell named: *MartinLutherKingDay.*

> In: *Lesson 3-2: Define range names for the calendar control settings,* you defined a range name by typing it directly into the *Name Box.*
>
> This time you will use a different technique.
>
> 1.　Click: Formulas→Defined Names→Define Name.
>
> > Note that Excel is proposing to create a range name called: _16_Jan_2017.
>
> 2.　Click in the *Name* box.
>
> 3.　Type: **MartinLutherKingDay**
>
> 4.　Click: OK.

5　Define range names for *PresidentsDay, LaborDay, ColumbusDay, ThanksgivingDay* and *MemorialDay.*

6　Check your range names using the Name Manager.

> Click: Formulas→Defined Names→Name Manager.
>
> The *Name Manager* dialog appears showing all of your defined names. If there are any errors, you can correct them using the *Edit* button.

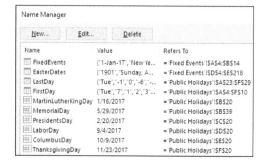

7   Add references to the FixedEvents table for each of the new range names.

   1.   Select the *Fixed Events* worksheet.

   2.   Click in cell B8.

   3.   Press the **<Tab>** key. This creates a new table row and moves the selected cell to cell A9.

   4.   Type: **=MartinLutherKingDay**

   5.   Press the **<Tab>** key. This should move the selected cell to cell B9. If it doesn't, press the **<Enter>** key and then move to cell B9 manually.

   6.   Type: **Martin Luther King day**

   7.   Press the **<Tab>** key. This creates a new table row and moves the selected cell to cell A10.

   8.   Continue until all of the public holidays have been added to the *FixedEvents* table.

8   Sort the table of Fixed Events by the Date column.

This isn't necessary, but it makes the table look tidy. If you add more entries to the table in the future they will not automatically re-sort.

   1.   Click in the *Date* column of the *FixedEvents* table.

   2.   Click: Data→Sort & Filter→Sort A-Z.

9   Check that all values are correctly calculated.

If you have selected 2017 as the current year (on the *Calendar* worksheet) you should see the fixed events dates shown in the sidebar.

10   Check that all of the fixed events are now displaying correctly on the *Calendar* worksheet.

11   Save the workbook as *Year Planner-31*.

Blank page

5

Session Five: Implement custom events

> There are many events in the womb of time, which will be delivered.
>
> *William Shakespeare, English playwright (1564 - 1616).*

In this session, you'll add custom events to the calendar.

Custom events are events that can be added by the user and will appear on the calendar.

Custom events can be defined as recurring or non-recurring. Recurring events will appear on every year of the calendar, while non-recurring events will only appear on the selected year.

Session Objectives

By the end of this session you will have:

- Linked non-recurring custom events to the calendar
- Prevented two non-recurring custom events from occurring on the same day
- Set up recurring custom events
- Linked recurring custom events to the calendar
- Prevented two recurring custom events from occurring on the same day
- Restricted the length of custom events

Lesson 5-1: Link non-recurring custom events to the calendar

In this lesson, you'll add formulas to the calendar to display non-recurring custom events.

You created the table that stores these in: *Lesson 2-12: Create a table for non-recurring custom events.*

1   Open *Year Planner-31* (if it isn't already open).

2   Select the *Calendar* worksheet if it isn't already selected.

3   Add a VLOOKUP function to cell F6 that will retrieve any non-recurring events for the date shown in cell F4.

Enter the following formula in cell F6:

=VLOOKUP(F4,CustomEvents,2,FALSE)

This works in exactly the same way as the VLOOKUP formula that you created for fixed events in: *Lesson 4-2: Link the table of fixed events to the calendar*. This time you're searching for the date (obtained from cell F4) within the *CustomEvents* table, and returning the value found in column 2: the name of the event.

The VLOOKUP function looks for the date (obtained from cell F4) in the left-hand column of the *CustomEvents* table. If a date is found, the value in column 2 of the *CustomEvents* table (the name of the event) is returned.

When you enter this formula in cell F6, you'll get the result: *#N/A*.

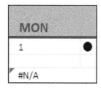

This happened because the VLOOKUP function couldn't find any custom events for this date.

You'll need to revise this formula exactly as you did for the fixed events formula in: *Lesson 4-2: Link the table of fixed events to the calendar*.

4   Revise the formula to suppress error messages.

Revise the formula to:

=IFERROR(VLOOKUP(F4,CustomEvents,2,FALSE),"")

This time the formula works correctly and nothing is shown in cell F6.

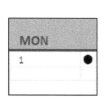

5   Revise the formula to respect the *Show Custom Events* setting.

You'll remember that the user needs to be able to show and hide custom events using the checkbox in the bottom left corner of the calendar.

To make this possible, revise the formula to:

=IF(ShowCustomEvents=TRUE, IFERROR(VLOOKUP(F4,CustomEvents,2,FALSE),""),"")

Year Planner-31

The additional IF function checks whether the value in the *ShowCustomEvents* control setting is TRUE or FALSE. If it's FALSE, it returns a blank cell.

You created the *ShowCustomEvents* control setting in: *Lesson 3-2: Define range names for the calendar control settings.*

6 **Fill the formula across to row S.**

1. Select cell F6.

2. Click and drag the fill handle to the right, all the way to cell R6.

Nothing appears in the cells, but if you click in each cell and check the Formula Bar, you'll see that the formula has been transferred correctly.

7 **Copy the formulas from row 6 to the other fixed events rows.**

1. Select cells F6:S6.

2. Copy the selected cells by pressing **<Ctrl> + <C>** or clicking Home→Clipboard→Copy.

3. Paste into cells F9, F12, F15 and F18.

If prompted to replace existing data, click *Yes*.

Most of the formulas are now in place, but cells F21 and H21 still don't have a formula for custom events. Cells F21 and H21 are merged cells that span 2 columns and 4 rows, while the other custom events cells span 2 columns and only 1 row.

It's a quirk of Excel that you're not able to copy and paste between merged cells unless they are merged in exactly the same way, so you will need to enter the formulas into these cells manually.

8 **Manually enter the formulas for cells F21 and H21.**

1. Enter the following formula in cell F21:

   =IF(ShowCustomEvents=TRUE, IFERROR(VLOOKUP(F19,CustomEvents,2,FALSE),""),"")

2. Copy cell F21 and paste into cell H21.

   Cells F21 and H21 are merged in the same way, so you will be able to copy and paste between them.

All of the formulas are now in place to display the custom events defined in the *CustomEvents* table on the *Custom Events* worksheet.

9 **Test the custom events by checking that *Dentist's Appointment* appears correctly.**

Use the calendar controls to select Jan-2016.

Dentist's Appointment appears correctly on the 2-Jan-2016. This proves that the non-recurring custom events are working correctly.

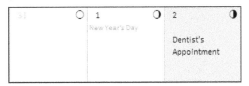

10 **Save the workbook as *Year Planner-32*.**

Lesson 5-2: Prevent two non-recurring custom events from occurring on the same day

The function specification requires:

4.1. It must be possible for a user to quickly define several custom events for each day (such as a birthday, holiday or appointment).

4.2. Events must be restricted to the visible space available for display for each calendar day without scrolling.

4.3. It must be possible to define custom events that are up to 32 characters (in total) long for each day.

The easiest solution would appear to be to allow the user to create multiple rows in the *CustomEvents* table with the same date. In this way the user could define several custom events for the same day.

Unfortunately, the VLOOKUP function cannot return values from more than one row in a table. When a match is found, VLOOKUP ignores all subsequent rows.

It is thus necessary to prevent the user from adding two rows to the *CustomEvents* table that have the same date. In this lesson you'll do this by adding a *unique constraint* to the *CustomEvents* table's *Date* column.

Users will be able to define multiple events for a single date by creating just one row and defining each event name within this row using the **<Alt> + <Enter>** key combination.

1   Open *Year Planner-32* (if it isn't already open).

2   Select the *Custom Events* worksheet if it isn't already selected.

3   Apply a validation rule to prevent two events from being entered to the *CustomEvents* table for the same date.

1.   Select cells A6:A7.

2.   Click: Data→Data Tools→Data Validation.

The *Data Validation* dialog appears.

3.   Click the *Allow* dropdown and select *Custom*.

4.   In the *Formula* box, enter:

=COUNTIF($A$6:$A7,$A6)=1

note

COUNTIF and COUNTIFS

The COUNTIF function returns a number indicating how many cells in a range match the given criteria.

COUNTIF works great when you need only one criteria, but it won't work if you need to use multiple criteria. The solution is to use COUNTIFS.

COUNTIFS allows you to not only select more than one criteria, but also to select more than one range of cells to count.

The SUMIF function also has a similar counterpart called SUMIFS.

SUMIF and SUMIFS work in exactly the same way as COUNTIF and COUNTIFS, except that the SUM functions add values together instead of counting them.

Excel 2019 also has MAXIFS and MINIFS functions to return maximum and minimum values based upon multiple criteria. These functions are new in Excel 2019 and won't work in earlier versions of Excel.

The COUNTIF function returns a number indicating how many cells it found that match its criteria. In this case, it's checking how many of the dates in column A match the date that was entered.

If there is only one instance of the date in column B, the COUNTIF function will return 1. Validation rules are processed after the value is entered in the cell, so a result of 1 means that the entered date doesn't exist already.

A result of 2 (or any other number) means that the date already exists, meaning it is not a valid entry.

This formula will only allow the date to be entered if the COUNTIF function returns 1, meaning that the same date cannot be entered twice.

5. Click: OK to close the dialog.

4   Test the validation rule.

1. Click in cell A8 and attempt to re-enter: **02-Jan-2016**

2. Press the **<Enter>** key.

An error dialog appears, showing that the date is invalid.

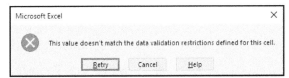

You'll make this error message more informative and user friendly later, in: *Lesson 7-1: Create user-friendly validation messages.*

3. Click *Cancel*.

4. Change the date in cell A8 to: **12-Jan-16**

This time the date is accepted, because it doesn't already exist within column A of the *CustomEvents* table.

Notice that there's now a potential conflict between the *Test Event* and *Jimmy's Birthday*, because they will both occur on the same day in 2016.

You'll deal with this later, in: *Lesson 5-4: Link recurring custom events to the calendar.*

5. Enter **Test Event** in cell B8.

5   Save the workbook as *Year Planner-33*.

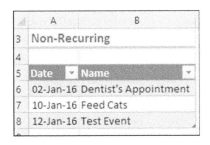

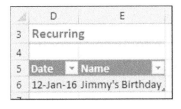

Lesson 5-3: Set up recurring custom events

You created the table for recurring custom events in: *Lesson 2-13: Create a table for recurring custom events.*

Recurring events happen on the same date each year. To make this possible, you're going to create a new column that modifies the dates of recurring events so that they always appear in the current year.

1   Open *Year Planner-33* (if it isn't already open).

2   Select the *Custom Events* worksheet if it isn't already selected.

3   Add a new column to the *RecurringEvents* table to the left of the *Date* column.

    1.   Right click in cell D6.

    2.   Click: Insert→Table Columns to the Left, from the shortcut menu.

    3.   In cell D5, type: **LookupKey** and then press the **<Enter>** key.

    4.   Resize all of the table columns so that they are the correct size for their contents.

4   Move the *RecurringEvents* table's title from cell D3 to cell E3.

In the final version of the year planner the *LookupKey* column will be hidden from the user. For this reason, the title should appear in column E.

    1.   Click in cell D3 to select it.

    2.   Move the mouse cursor to the border of the selected cell until you see the four-headed arrow cursor shape.

It is a quirk of Excel that you can't move a merged cell directly into an area that overlaps its original location. This means that you can't move the title directly to cells E3:F3.

Instead, you'll move it to the row above and then move it down to the correct location.

    3.   When you see the four-headed arrow, click and drag to move the title to cells E2:F2.

    4.   After moving the title to row 2, click and drag again to move the merged cell into cells E3:F3.

Year Planner-33

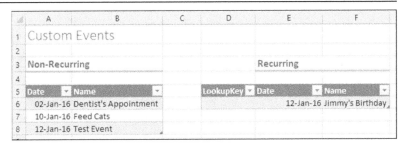

5   Create a formula in the *LookupKey* column that will modify recurring events to always appear in the same year.

1.   Click in cell D6 to select it.

2.   Enter the following formula:

=DATE(0,MONTH([Date]),DAY([Date]))

This formula uses the DATE function to remove the *Year* part of the date and replace it with a zero, indicating the year 1900. Recurring events will be shown every year, so reassigning them all to the same year will make it easier to link them to the calendar.

[Date] is a Structured Table Reference. These allow you to refer to a certain column within a table no matter which row the formula is on. Structured Table References make formulas easier to understand and less prone to error.

6   Make sure that the formula is filled down correctly.

By default, Excel tables automatically fill formulas into the other cells in the same column.

You've already seen this behaviour, in: *Lesson 4-3: Add fixed-date national holidays.*

1.   In cell E7, enter: **04-Jul-2016**

2.   In cell F7, enter: **Forrest's Birthday**

The formula in column D should automatically fill down to create the date: **04-Jul-00.**

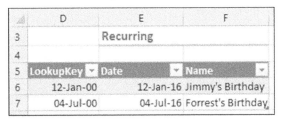

See sidebar if the formula in cell D6 didn't automatically fill down to cell D7.

7   Save the workbook as *Year Planner-34.*

note

Calculated columns

Calculated columns allow Tables to automatically fill down formulas when a new row is added to the table.

This extremely useful feature makes it possible for your Table to automatically generate a *LookupKey* every time a new record is added to the recurring events table.

It's easy to accidentally disable this feature, so you may need to re-enable it if it isn't working for you.

To do this:

1. Click: File→Options→Proofing→ AutoCorrect Options→ AutoFormat As You Type

2. Make sure that *Fill formulas in tables to create calculated columns* is checked.

3. Click *OK* twice to close both dialogs.

note

ASCII

ASCII (pronounced Askey) is an acronym for: *American Standard Code for Information Interchange.*

In 1968, the US President (Lyndon B. Johnson) ordered that all computers purchased by the United States Federal Government must support ASCII.

ASCII defines a number (between 0 and 127) for the numbers **0-9**, lowercase letters **a** to **z**, uppercase letters **A** to **Z**, basic punctuation symbols, the space character, and 33 non-printable control characters (many of which are now obsolete).

For example, the ASCII code for an upper-case **A** character is 65.

Excel has two ASCII related functions:

CHAR(number)

This function returns an ASCII character from the corresponding ASCII code. For example:

=CHAR(65)

… would result in an upper-case **A** character appearing in the cell.

CODE(text)

This function returns an ASCII code number from a character. For example:

=CODE("A")

… would return the number 65 (the ASCII code number for an upper-case A).

Lesson 5-4: Link recurring custom events to the calendar

In *Lesson 5-2: Prevent two non-recurring custom events from occurring on the same day,* you prevented the user from entering two non-recurring custom events on the same date.

This will work correctly, but it won't prevent the user from entering a recurring event for the same date.

You'll fix this by enabling the calendar to display a single recurring event and a single non-recurring event on each day.

1 Open *Year Planner-34* (if it isn't already open).

2 Select the *Calendar* worksheet if it isn't selected already.

3 Modify the formula in the calendar to allow recurring events to appear on the same day as non-recurring events.

1. Return to the *Calendar* worksheet.

2. In cell F6, enter the following formula:

   **=IF(ShowCustomEvents=TRUE,
   IFERROR(VLOOKUP(F4,CustomEvents,2,FALSE)
   &CHAR(10),"")
   &IFERROR(VLOOKUP(DATE(0,MONTH(F4),DAY(F4)),
   RecurringEvents,3,FALSE),""),"")**

   This formula looks very complicated, but it's almost exactly the same as the one you created in: *Lesson 5-1: Link non-recurring custom events to the calendar.*

   Instead of using a single VLOOKUP function to return a single event from the *CustomEvents* table, you're now using two VLOOKUP functions to first search for non-recurring events in the *CustomEvents* table and then search for recurring events in the *RecurringEvents* table.

   The VLOOKUP function for recurring events replaces the year of the calendar date with a zero, enabling it to match the *LookupKey* column that you created in: *Lesson 5-3: Set up recurring custom events.*

   You're using the & symbol to concatenate the two results together, so that they will both appear within the same cell.

   All letters, numbers and other symbols have a unique character code. The *CHAR* function allows you to specify a code and extract the corresponding character. Character code 10 is the code for a line break.

   By using &CHAR(10), you're adding a line break between the two VLOOKUP functions so that the events will appear on separate lines.

4 Copy the formulas to all of the other custom events cells.

Do this in the same way as you did in *Lesson 5-1: Link non-recurring custom events to the calendar.*

Year Planner-34

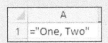
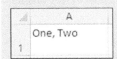
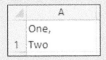

Copy the formula from cell F6 to all of the other custom events cells except cells F21 and H21.

Remember that you won't be able to copy and paste into cells F21 and H21 and will have to enter the formula into these cells manually.

The formula for cell F21 should be:

=IF(ShowCustomEvents=TRUE, IFERROR(VLOOKUP(F19,CustomEvents,2,FALSE) &CHAR(10),"") &IFERROR(VLOOKUP(DATE(0,MONTH(F19),DAY(F19)), RecurringEvents,3,FALSE),""),"")

When you've entered this formula into cell F21 you can copy it into cell H21.

5   **Test the new formula.**

1.   Select the *Calendar* tab.

2.   Set the date to: **Jan-2016**

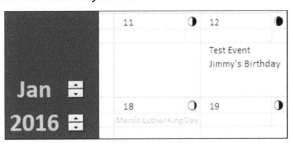

Test Event and *Jimmy's Birthday* are now visible on the same day.

3.   Set the date to: **Jan-2017**

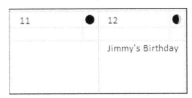

Jimmy's Birthday still appears on the 12-Jan-2017. This is correct, because it is a recurring event that appears every year.

Test Event doesn't appear in 2017 because it is a non-recurring event. It only appears on 21-Jul-2016.

6   **Save the workbook as *Year Planner-35*.**

Lesson 5-5: Prevent two recurring custom events from occurring on the same day

You've now implemented both recurring and non-recurring custom events, and you have also prevented any non-recurring events from being entered for the same date.

In the context of a recurring event, the year entered for the event is redundant. The LookupKey column essentially ignores any year entered by the user.

This opens up the possibility of a conflict if the user enters two recurring events that have the same day and month (even though the years may differ).

If this happens, the two events will conflict and one of them will not be displayed.

1   Open *Year Planner-35* (if it isn't already open).

2   Add a conflicting recurring event.

    1.   Select the *Custom Events* worksheet if it isn't selected already.

    2.   In cell E8, enter: **12-Jan-17**

    3.   In cell F8, enter: **Winter Festival**

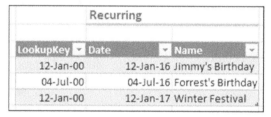

    The formula in the *LookupKey* column should automatically fill down. If it doesn't, refer to: *Lesson 5-3: Set up recurring custom events*.

    Notice that, even though *Jimmy's Birthday* and *Winter Festival* have been entered with different years, they both have an identical *LookupKey*.

    4.   Select the *Calendar* worksheet and switch to Jan 2017 if it isn't already selected.

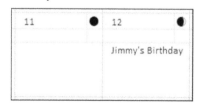

    Jimmy's Birthday appears, but *Summer Festival* doesn't.

    It is not possible for two recurring events to be displayed on the same day, so you'll need to add a validation rule to prevent this.

Year Planner-35

3 Apply a validation rule to prevent two recurring events from being entered for the same date.

1. Return to the *Custom Events* worksheet.

2. Select cells E6:E8.

3. Click Data→Data Tools→Data Validation.

   The *Data Validation* dialog appears.

4. Click the *Allow* dropdown and select *Custom*.

5. In the *Formula* box, enter:

   =COUNTIF($D$6:$D8,$D6)=1

6. Click: OK.

   This is very similar to the validation rule that you created in: *Lesson 5-2: Prevent two non-recurring custom events from occurring on the same day*. The only difference is that you are checking for duplicate values in the *LookupKey* column instead of the *Date* column.

   If you look at the table, you can see why this is necessary:

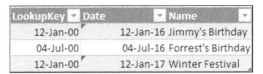

   Even though *Jimmy's Birthday* and *Winter Festival* have been entered with different years, they both have the same month and year, producing a duplicate value in the *LookupKey* column.

4 Test the validation rule.

1. Click in cell E8 and attempt to re-enter: **12-Jan-2017**

   An error dialog appears, showing that the date is invalid.

   You'll make this error message more informative and user friendly later, in: *Lesson 7-1: Create user-friendly validation messages*.

2. Click *Cancel*.

3. Change the date in cell A8 to: **11-Jan-2017**

   This time the date is accepted, because it doesn't conflict with any of the other recurring events.

5 Save the workbook as *Year Planner-36*.

Lesson 5-6: Restrict the length of custom events

The custom events system is now completely functional, but there's one more requirement stated in the functional specification that hasn't been addressed.

4.2. Events must be restricted to the visible space available for display for each calendar day without scrolling.

4.3. It must be possible to define custom events that are up to 32 characters (in total) long for each day.

There's a limited amount of space in each cell on the calendar, but the user can currently enter an unlimited amount of text for each event. It is necessary to prevent users from entering more text than can fit in each of the calendar's date boxes.

1   Open *Year Planner-36* (if it isn't already open).

2   Select the *Custom Events* worksheet if it isn't already selected.

3   Test the capacity of the calendar cells by entering a very long custom event name.

1.   In cell B7, replace *Feed Cats* with 32 letter W's:

WWWWWWWWWWWWWWWWWWWWWWW (x32)

A capital W is the widest letter in the alphabet, so it is the best letter to choose when testing the number of characters that can fit in a cell.

2.   Select the *Calendar* worksheet.

3.   Switch to Jan-2016 if it isn't selected already.

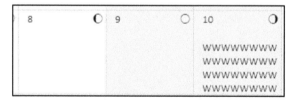

You can now see the custom event 10-Jan.

There are 4 rows within the cell, each containing 8 instances of the letter W. This means that the 32 characters specified in the functional specification will fit into each cell.

4   Add validation rules to prevent more than 32 characters from being entered for each custom event.

1.   Return to the *Custom Events* worksheet.

2.   Select cells B6:B8.

3.   Click: Data→Data Tools→Data Validation.

The *Data Validation* dialog appears.

4.   Click the *Allow* dropdown and select *Text length*.

Year Planner-36

note

Making the text length validation perfectly comply with the functional specification

This lesson's implementation is not perfect. As noted in the lesson:

It would still be possible for the user to enter more text than can fit in a calendar cell by entering both recurring and non-recurring events for the same date.

There is a solution to this problem but it involves a complex formula-driven custom validation. Here's how you could implement it:

1. Add a new column to the left of column C, titled: **Total Length**.

2. In cell C6, enter the formula:

=LEN((B6)&IFERROR(VLOOKUP(DATE(0, MONTH(A6),DAY(A6)), RecurringEvents,3,FALSE),""))

This formula extracts any recurring events that correspond to the same date and calculates the total combined length of both events.

3. Select cells B6:B8.

2. Click: Data→Data Tools→ Data Validation.

3. Click the *Allow* drop-down list and select *Custom*.

4. A formula box appears. The validation will fail if the expression entered into this box returns FALSE.

The validation you need is: **=C6<=32**

This will prevent the user from entering a non-recurring custom event if the resulting text exceeds 32 characters in length.

Cells F6:F8 can be validated in the same way by adding a *Total Length* column in column H with a similar formula.

5. Click the *Data* dropdown and select *less than or equal to*.

6. In the *Maximum* box, type: **32**

7. Click *OK*.

5 Apply the same validation rule to cells F6:F8.

6 Test the new validation rule.

1. In cell B7, enter:
   ABCDEFGHIJKLMNOPQRSTUVWXYZ1234567

   This is 33 characters long, so it won't be accepted by your validation rule.

   You'll make this error message more informative and user friendly later, in: *Lesson 7-1: Create user-friendly validation messages*.

2. Change the value in cell B7 to:

   ABCDEFGHIJKLMNOPQRSTUVWXYZ123456

   This time you are only entering 32 characters, so the value is accepted.

3. Resize column B to be wide enough for its contents.

4. Resize column F to be the same width (about 270 pixels).

Your text length validations are now complete. They are not completely perfect, but you'd need to take a view upon whether they are "good enough". It is still possible for the user to enter more text than can fit in a calendar cell by entering both recurring and non-recurring events for the same date.

There is a solution to this problem, but it involves a rather long custom validation expression. This solution is shown in the sidebar.

7 Save the workbook as *Year Planner-37*.

Blank page

Session Six: Implement moon phases

Most readers will be familiar with the *Full Moon* (when the shape of the moon looks like a full circle).

After each full moon the shape of the moon gradually changes, until it returns to a full moon after approximately 29.5 days (a lunar month).

Ancient civilizations used lunar calendars that were based entirely upon the observed shape of the moon. Man-made lunar calendars have been discovered that could be as much as 32,000 years old.

Solar calendars (that are based upon the earth's rotation around the sun) are more useful than lunar calendars, as they remain in synchronization with the seasons of the year. The calendar that is most widely used today (and the calendar used in this project) is the Gregorian solar calendar (defined by Pope Gregory XIII in 1582).

In Western culture eight different phases (or moon shapes) are generally recognized. In this session you will add appropriate icons to the calendar that will indicate the correct phase of the moon for each day.

Accurately calculating the phase of the moon for each date (in the solar calendar) is a very complex task. To calculate the moon phases with 100% accuracy would involve extremely complex formulas that plot the orbit of the moon.

In this session you'll calculate the correct phase of the moon (and display an appropriate icon) for every date in the calendar.

Session Objectives

By the end of this session you will have:

■ Created a worksheet for moon phases

■ Calculated the moon's age

■ Calculated the phase of the moon based on the moon's age

■ Linked the moon phases to the calendar

Lesson 6-1: Create a worksheet for moon phases

In this lesson, you'll create a worksheet with a Table to store the moon phase calculations for an entire year.

1   Open *Year Planner-37* (if it isn't already open).

2   Set the Calendar year to 2016.

3   Add a new worksheet named **Moon Phases**.

   1.   Click the *New sheet* icon below the worksheet: ⊞

       A new worksheet appears.

   2.   Right click the new worksheet and click *Rename* from the shortcut menu.

   3.   Type **Moon Phases** and press <Enter>.

4   Add a title in cell A1 with the text: **Moon Phase Calculation**

   1.   Click in cell A1 and enter: **Moon Phase Calculation**

   2.   Apply the *Title* style to cell A1.

5   Add a table to the *Moon Phases* worksheet containing an entire year of dates.

   1.   Select the *Moon Phases* worksheet.

   2.   In cell A3, type: **Date**

   3.   In cell A4, type the formula: **=DATE(CalendarYear,1,1)**

   4.   Press the **<Enter>** key.

       This returns 01-Jan for the currently selected year. Because the selected year is 2016, the date *01-Jan-16* is returned.

   5.   In cell A5, enter the formula: **=A4+1**

       This simply adds one day to the previous date.

   6.   Press the **<Enter>** key.

   7.   AutoFill the formula in cell A5 down to cell A369.

       You are going to use these dates to calculate the phases of the moon for every date possible for the calendar's selected year.

       Notice that you've created 366 dates instead of 365. This is to account for leap years. The year 2016 is a leap year, so the 31st of December 2016 appears in cell A369.

6   Add six dates to the end of the range to allow for the calendar's overlap.

   You'll remember that each month on the calendar can potentially overlap into the next and previous months. This means that it's possible for up to 6 days to be visible on the calendar from the next and previous years.

   Select cell A369 and AutoFill down to cell A375.

Year Planner-37

This accounts for the possible overlap at the end of December.

7   Add six extra dates to the beginning of the range to allow for the calendar's underlap.

1. Select rows 4-9.

2. Right-click inside the selected area.

3. Click: *Insert* from the shortcut menu.

   Six blank rows are added to the beginning of the range.

4. In cell A9, enter the formula: **=A10-1**

   This will subtract one day from the date in cell A10.

5. Press the **<Enter>** key.

   The date *31-Dec-15* appears in cell A9 because that is one day before 01-Jan-16 (the currently selected year).

6. AutoFill the formula from cell A9 up to cell A4.

   This accounts for the possible underlap before the beginning of January.

8   Convert the range of dates into a Table.

A Table will make the moon phase data easier to refer to in formulas, as well as making the calculation formulas easier to create and work with.

You first created a Table in: *Lesson 2-12: Create a table for non-recurring custom events.*

1. Click anywhere within the list of dates.

2. Click Insert→Tables→Table.

   The Create Table dialog appears.

3. Make sure that *My table has headers* is checked.

4. Click *OK*.

9   Name the new table: **MoonPhaseData**

1. Click: Table Tools→Design→Properties→Table Name.

2. Type: **MoonPhaseData**

3. Press the **<Enter>** key.

10   Remove the filter arrows from the table.

Click: Data→Sort & Filter→Filter.

11   Save the workbook as *Year Planner-38*.

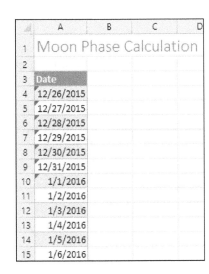

note

Accurately calculating the moon's age

Calculating the moon's age with 100% accuracy would require some very complex formulas that plot the orbit of the moon.

In this lesson you use the date of a known new moon to calculate the moon phases since that date. This is a very easy calculation, but it becomes less accurate as the dates get further away from the last known new moon.

You can increase the accuracy of the calculation by using a known new moon that is closer to the date you are calculating the moon phase for.

There are also several other formulas that can calculate the phases of the moon more accurately without plotting the moon's orbit, but they are a lot more complex and still not 100% accurate.

The simple formula used in this lesson should be sufficient for most purposes that don't require 100% accuracy.

trivia

Different types of lunar months

When calculating the phases of the month, this book uses the *synodic month*. This is a type of lunar month.

There are five different types of lunar month, all calculated in different ways. They are the Sidereal Month, Tropical Month, Anomalistic Month and Draconic Month.

Year Planner-38

Lesson 6-2: Calculate the moon's age

The moon's age

Moon phases are calculated according to the 'age' of the moon. The age of the moon is defined as:

The number of days since the last new moon.

There are eight phases of the moon (beginning with the *New* moon) that repeat (in sequence) on average every 29.5 days (this is called a *synodic month*).

This means that if you know the precise date of a single New Moon, you can calculate the date of the next New Moon by simply adding one *synodic month* to this date. You can also calculate the dates of every future New Moon using the same interval.

The functional specification calls for the calendar to support dates from 1916 to 2116, so the best starting point for the calculation is the first new moon that is on or before 01-Jan-1916.

The closest new moon on or before 01-Jan-1916 occurred on 06-Dec-1915.

Calculating the number of days since the new moon of 06-Dec-1915

Excel's system of *date serial numbers* makes this incredibly simple. The concept of date serial numbers was introduced in: *Lesson 3-5: Create helper cells to determine the calendar start date.*

The date serial number for 06-Dec-1915 is 5819. This means that you can calculate the number of days since 06-Dec-1915 by subtracting 5819 from the date serial number of any date since then.

Calculating the moon's age

Because you now know the number of elapsed days since the new moon of 06-Dec-1915, you can calculate the age of the moon by using Excel's MOD function. The MOD function has the syntax:

MOD(number, divisor)

The function returns the remainder (sometimes called the modulus) after a number is divided by divisor. For example:

=MOD(16,7)

… would return the number 2 because sixteen can be divided by seven twice with a remainder or two.

This function makes it easy to determine the age of the moon as you already know that there was a new moon on 06-Dec-1915 (date serial number 5819). The formula:

=MOD([Date] - 5819, 29.5)

© 2018 The Smart Method® Ltd

note

If your table didn't automatically AutoFill somebody has switched calculated columns off

Calculated Columns allow Tables to automatically fill down formulas when a new row is added to the table.

It's easy to accidentally disable this (extremely useful) feature, so you may need to re-enable it if it isn't working for you.

To do this:

1. Click:

File→Options→Proofing→ AutoCorrect Options→ AutoFormat As You Type

2. Make sure that *Fill formulas in tables to create calculated columns* is checked.

3. Click *OK* twice to close both dialogs.

trivia

The mean length of a synodic month

The word synodic comes from the Greek word for a meeting or assembly. In this context the meeting is between the sun and the moon.

A synodic month is often referred to as being 29.5 days in duration. While this is a rough average, synodic months can range from around 29.18 to 29.93 days.

There are many ways of calculating the mean length of a synodic month.

In this lesson you have used a generally-accepted mean length of **29.530588853** days.

The true synodic month can vary from this mean value by up to seven hours.

… will therefore return the age of the moon for any date. In this lesson you will use a more precise definition for the average synodic month (29.530588853 days).

1   Open *Year Planner-38* (if it isn't already open).

2   Select the *Moon Phases* worksheet if it isn't already selected.

3   Add a column to the MoonPhaseData table, called: **Age**

1.   Click in cell B3 and type: **Age**

2.   Press the **<Enter>** key.

4   Add a formula to column B that will calculate the age of the moon.

Enter the following formula into cell B4:

=MOD([Date]-5819,29.530588853)

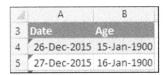

Excel should AutoFill the formula to every other cell in column B. If this doesn't happen for you somebody has switched calculated columns off in your copy of Excel. See sidebar for instructions upon how to switch it back on.

Also notice that Excel has incorrectly formatted the result of the formula as a date.

5   Apply the Comma style to the result of the formula.

1.   Click the column B header to select all of the cells in the column.

2.   Click: Home→Number→Comma Style.

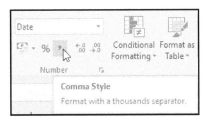

You can now see that on the 26th of December 2015, the moon was 15.66 days old. This places it between the *full moon* and *waning gibbous* phases.

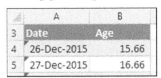

6   Save the workbook as *Year Planner-39*.

anecdote

The wisdom of making things "good enough"

In this lesson you've calculated the phase of the moon to an accuracy of around seven hours which is deemed to be "good enough". You could, of course, have taken a lookup table-based approach (as you did in: *Lesson 4-8: Calculate the date for Easter Sunday*) for perfectly precise values.

Many years ago, I was asked to specify an electronic document management system for a large finance company. The system centrally stored scanned finance documents and rapidly displayed them on help desk personnel's computer screens. It was important that the system was very reliable as the entire helpdesk operation would grind to a halt if it were to fail.

At a meeting to determine the functional specification, I was told that the system must have "99.99% uptime". This was quite a challenge as it meant less than an hour's downtime each year. 99.99% was achievable but at great cost. Every part of the system had to be engineered with 100% redundancy (2 of everything).

When the directors received the unexpected high hardware cost estimate, I explained the challenges of 99.99% uptime, mentioning that only 99% uptime would result in less than half the hardware cost.

The directors smiled and said that 99% would be fine. The 99.99% figure had not been researched in any way but just plucked out of the air. Really, they wanted the system to just be "good enough".

Year Planner-39

Lesson 6-3: Calculate the phase of the moon based on the moon's age

In this lesson, you'll calculate the phases of the moon using a very simple formula. The formula isn't precisely accurate but should be accurate to around plus or minus seven hours. If you needed the phases of the moon to be more precise you could use the same technique you employed in: *Lesson 4-8: Calculate the date for Easter Sunday* to obtain precise values.

1   Open *Year Planner-39* (if it isn't already open).

2   Select the *Moon Phases* worksheet if it isn't already selected.

3   Add data for the moon phase symbols.

Now that you have calculated the age of the moon, you need to link these ages to the moon's different phases. You'll do that by adding another table.

1.   In cell D3, enter: **Age**

2.   In cell E3, enter: **Phase**

3.   In cell D4, enter the following formula:

=(ROW()-4)*(29.530588853/8)

The ROW function returns the row number of the cell that the formula is placed in. In cell D4, this will be 4. You're subtracting 4 from this, resulting in 0.

You're then multiplying zero by the length of the lunar cycle (synodic month) divided by 8. This will allow you to extract the exact points at which the lunar cycle is divided into its 8 phases.

4.   Fill the formula in cell D4 down to cell D12.

5.   In column E, enter the symbols for each moon phase, starting and finishing with the new moon.

You learned how to insert the moon phase symbols in: *Lesson 2-9: Add moon phase symbols.*

You can also copy and paste these from the calendar.

	A	B	C	D	E
1	Moon Phase Calculation				
2					
3	Date	Age		Age	Phase
4	26-Dec-15	15.66		0	●
5	27-Dec-15	16.66		3.691324	◑
6	28-Dec-15	17.66		7.382647	◐
7	29-Dec-15	18.66		11.07397	○
8	30-Dec-15	19.66		14.76529	○
9	31-Dec-15	20.66		18.45662	◑
10	01-Jan-16	21.66		22.14794	◑
11	02-Jan-16	22.66		25.83927	◐
12	03-Jan-16	23.66		29.53059	●
13	04-Jan-16	24.66			

4 Convert the range containing the moon phases into a table.

1. Click in any cell within the moon phase data.

2. Click: Insert→Tables→Table.

   You are prompted to confirm creating the Table.

3. Make sure that *My table has headers* is checked and click *OK*.

5 Name the new table: **MoonPhases**

1. Click: Table Tools→Design→Properties→Table Name.

2. Type: **MoonPhases**

3. Press the **<Enter>** key.

6 Create a formula to extract the moon phase for each date.

1. Insert a new column to the left of column C.

2. In cell C3, type: **Moon Phase**

3. Resize column C to be wide enough for its contents.

4. In cell C4, enter the following formula:

   =VLOOKUP([Age],MoonPhases,2,TRUE)

   This formula uses an *inexact* VLOOKUP function to find the phase of the moon that is closest to the moon's age.

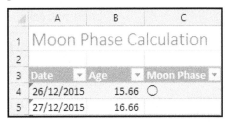

The correct phase of the moon appears next to every date in the table.

If your moon symbols do not automatically AutoFill somebody has switched calculated columns off in your copy of Excel. See: *Lesson 6-2: Calculate the moon's age (sidebar),* for instructions upon how to switch calculated columns back on.

Your moon symbols may look a little odd. This is because the default symbol font has been changed in Excel 2019. See sidebar for instructions upon how to reset the font to keep the moon symbols consistent.

7 Save the workbook as *Year Planner-40*.

note

If your moon icons look odd here's how to fix the problem

The moon symbols that you created in *Lesson 2-9: Add moon phase symbols* are part of the *Segoe UI Symbol* font. In Excel 2016 this was the default font for displaying symbols such as the ones you are using for the moon phases.

In Excel 2019, the new *Segoe UI Emoji* font is the default font for symbols. For this reason, the moon phases may look different in your *MoonPhaseData* table.

If this happens, you can keep your workbook consistent by changing the font in column C to *Segoe UI Symbol*.

Lesson 6-4: Link the moon phases to the calendar

Now that you've calculated the moon phases for each date, you can make them appear on the calendar in the same way as you did for the fixed events and custom events.

1   Open *Year Planner-40* (if it isn't already open).

2   Select the *Calendar* worksheet if it isn't already selected.

3   Use the calendar controls to display December 2016.

4   Set the calendar to use Sunday as the first day of the week and check all three check boxes.

5   Create a formula in cell G4 that will return the moon phase symbol for the date in cell F4.

   1.   Type the following formula into cell G4:

   **=IF(ShowMoonPhases,
   VLOOKUP(F4,MoonPhaseData,3,FALSE),"")**

   This formula uses a VLOOKUP function in combination with an IF function. You used a similar formula in: *Lesson 4-2: Link the table of fixed events to the calendar.*

   The formula searches the *MoonPhaseData* table for the date appearing in the adjacent cell and then returns the symbol that appears in column 3 of the table (the icon of the correct moon phase for this date).

   2.   Press the **<Enter>** key.

   The correct moon phase icon for 27th of November 2016 is shown in cell G4. In this case it is a *waning crescent*.

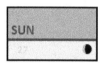

6   Copy the formula in cell G4

   1.   Click in cell G4.

   2.   Press the **<Ctrl>+<C>** keys to copy the formula.

7   Paste the formula into all the other moon phase cells on the calendar.

   You need to be very careful while doing this, as the formulas on the calendar can't be Auto Filled across. You couldn't, for example, select cells F4:G4 and AutoFill across, as this would break the formulas that calculate the dates.

   You also need to be careful when pasting into cells that contain conditional formats, as this can cause them to be corrupted.

   The cells containing the moon symbols are very small, so you may wish to zoom in to make it easier to select them (see sidebar).

   1.   Hold down the **<Ctrl>** key on your keyboard.

tip

Zooming in

This lesson requires you to select some very small cells. In such cases, it can be useful to zoom in.

You can zoom in and out by holding down the **<Ctrl>** key and rolling the wheel on your mouse.

Alternatively, you can use the zoom control in the bottom-right corner of the Excel window.

Year Planner-40

2. With **<Ctrl>** held down, click each of the calendar cells that contain the moon phase icons.

   Remember that Excel 2019 has a new feature that allows you to deselect cells if you make a mistake while selecting. This was covered in: *Lesson 3-11: Add conditional formatting for the moon phases (sidebar).*

3. Click: Home→Clipboard→Paste→Formulas.

   Formulas are pasted into all of the moon phase cells without affecting any other formulas or conditional formats.

8 **Test the moon phases**.

1. Use the calendar controls to display July 2016.

   You should see the moon phases changing as you change each month.

   Note that, if you have a slower computer, you may see some delay as you scroll through the calendar (see sidebar).

2. Confirm that the moon phases are correct.

   The calendar for July 2016 should appear as shown below:

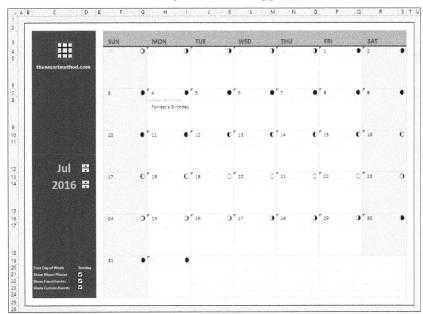

9 Save the workbook as *Year Planner-41*.

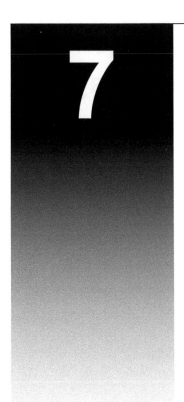

Session Seven: Finish the user interface

The year planner is now almost complete.

In this session you'll implement the last few features, tidy up the user interface and apply security.

By the end of this session, the year planner will be complete and ready to be distributed to your users.

At the end of this session you'll have a completed year planner. Because you fully understand how it works, you are equipped with the skills needed to continue to add more features to the year planner or to integrate it with other systems.

The year planner could be a useful part of almost any Excel application that makes use of dates.

Session Objectives

By the end of this session you will have:

- Created user-friendly validation messages
- Hidden error warnings and unlocked cells
- Hidden settings and applied protection
- Removed test data and finalized the year planner

note

The Stop, Warning and Info error alert styles

Windows users are conditioned to understand the meaning of three different icons.

Stop

 Something terrible has happened!

Warning

 Something quite bad has happened.

Information

 We just thought you'd like to know.

Each of these styles produces a slightly different error message dialog.

The *Warning* dialog shows four buttons (Yes, No, Cancel and Help) and the *Information* dialog shows just three buttons: OK, Cancel and Help.

The only important difference between them is that you cannot over-ride a *Stop* style, while the *Information* and *Warning* styles enable you to dismiss the warning and enter an invalid value.

Because you do not want your users to ever over-ride the validations used in the Calendar and Year Planner application, the *Stop* style is the most appropriate.

Lesson 7-1: Create user-friendly validation messages

You've already created several validation rules, but the message that appears if an invalid value is entered is not very user friendly.

In this lesson, you'll make the validation messages more informative and useful to the user.

1 Open *Year Planner-41* (if it isn't already open).

2 Select the *Calendar* worksheet if it isn't already selected.

3 Apply a user-friendly validation message to cell D20.

Cell D20 currently contains a *List Validation* that requires either *Monday* or *Sunday* to be entered in the cell.

1. Click in cell D20 to select it.

2. Click: Data→Data Tools→Data Validation.

   The *Data Validation* dialog appears.

3. Click the *Error Alert* tab.

4. In the *Title* box, type: **Invalid Setting**

5. In the *Error Message* box, type:

   You may only set the first day of the week to Sunday or Monday.

6. Click *OK*.

4 Test the validation message.

1. In cell D20, type: **Test** and then press the **<Enter>** key.

The error message is displayed.

Year Planner-41

2. Click *Cancel* to revert the cell back to its previous value.

5 Select the *Custom Events* worksheet.

6 Apply a user-friendly validation message to cells A6:A8.

1. Select cells A6:A8.

2. Click: Data→Data Tools-->Data Validation.

   The *Data Validation* dialog appears.

3. Click on the *Error Alert* tab.

4. In the *Title* box, type: **Invalid Date**

5. In the *Error Message* box, type:

   A custom event already exists for this date. You cannot enter two non-recurring events for the same date, but you can enter multiple lines for a single date by pressing <Alt>+<Enter> to insert line breaks.

6. Click: *OK*.

7 Apply a user-friendly validation message to cells B6:B8.

1. Set the *Title* to: **Event name too long**

2. Set the *Error Message* to:

   Event names cannot exceed 32 characters.

8 Apply a user-friendly validation message to cells E6:E8.

1. Set the *Title* to: **Invalid Date**

   Set the *Error Message* to:

   A recurring event that will occur on this date already exists.

9 Apply a user-friendly validation message to cells F6:F8.

1. Set the *Title* to: **Event name too long**

2. Set the *Error Message* to:

   Event names cannot exceed 32 characters.

10 Save the workbook as *Year Planner-42*.

Lesson 7-2: Hide error warnings and unlock cells

You may have noticed that many of the cells on the calendar are marked with green triangles to indicate potential errors. You will hide those in this lesson.

You will also unlock some of the cells that contain important settings. This will enable them to continue working correctly after you protect the workbook later, in: *Lesson 7-3: Hide settings and apply protection*.

1   Open *Year Planner-42* (if it isn't already open).

2   Select the *Calendar* worksheet if it isn't already selected.

Notice that there are green triangles in the corners of many of the cells.

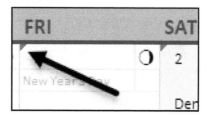

These are appearing because Excel suspects that you might have made a mistake with your formulas.

You haven't made any mistakes in this case, so you'll need to tell Excel to hide these.

3   Hide the error markers.

1. Select cells H4:S24.

This is the cell range that contains cells with the green triangle warnings.

2. Click the Smart Tag that appears to the top left of the selected cells and click *Ignore Error* from the shortcut menu.

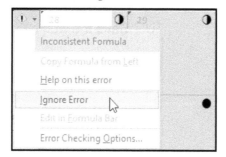

All of the green triangles disappear.

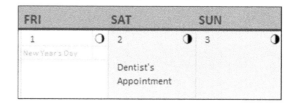

Year Planner-42

4 Unlock cell D20.

Cell D20 contains the setting for the first day of the week. This needs to be unlocked so that the user will still be able to change this setting after the worksheet is protected.

1. Right-click on cell D20 and click *Format Cells* from the shortcut menu.

2. Click the *Protection* tab.

3. Uncheck the *Locked* checkbox.

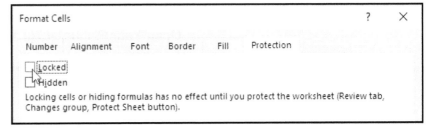

4. Click *OK*.

5 Unlock cells W2:W7.

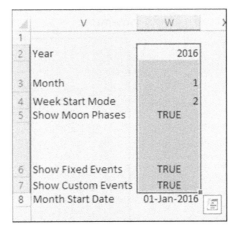

These are cells with values that can be changed by the controls on the calendar. You need to unlock them before protecting the worksheet or the controls will not work.

6 Save the workbook as *Year Planner-43*.

Lesson 7-3: Hide settings and apply protection

The calendar is now feature-complete, but there are a lot of settings and calculations that should be hidden from the user before distributing the year planner.

In this lesson you'll hide the inner workings of the year planner from the user and protect it to prevent the user from accidentally modifying any of the formulas.

1   Open *Year Planner-43* (if it isn't already open).

2   Select the *Calendar* worksheet if it isn't already selected.

3   Hide columns V and W.

Columns V and W contain the control settings that are used by the calendar. These should be hidden from the user.

1. Select columns V and W.

2. Right click in the selected area and click *Hide* from the shortcut menu.

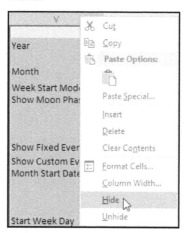

4   Hide the *Fixed Events, Public Holidays* and *Moon Phases* worksheets.

These worksheets contain data that most users would never need to change, so they should be hidden.

1. Click the *Fixed Events* worksheet tab to select it.

2. Hold down the **<Ctrl>** key.

3. Click on the *Public Holidays* worksheet tab.

4. Click on the *Moon Phases* worksheet tab.

5. Right-click on one of the selected tabs.

6. Click: *Hide* from the shortcut menu.

Year Planner-43

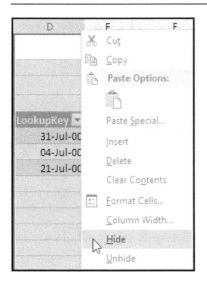

The *Fixed Events, Public Holidays* and *Moon Phases* worksheet tabs disappear.

5 Select the *Custom Events* worksheet.

6 Hide column D.

1. Select column D.

2. Right-click in the selected area.

3. Click: *Hide* from the shortcut menu.

This column contains the unique *LookupKey* value that you created in: *Lesson 5-3: Set up recurring custom events*. This should be hidden to avoid confusing your users.

7 Select the *Calendar* worksheet.

8 Protect the worksheet.

1. Click: Review→Protect→Protect Sheet.

(If you are using an older version of Excel the *Protect* group may be named *Changes*).

The *Protect Sheet* dialog appears.

2. Uncheck *Select locked cells* so that only *Select unlocked cells* is checked.

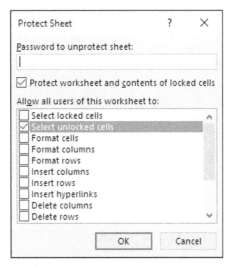

3. Click *OK*.

The *Calendar* worksheet is now protected. The user can still use the controls to change the calendar's settings, but can't accidentally change any of the formulas.

9 Save the workbook as *Year Planner-44*.

trivia

The reason that errors in computer code are called bugs is often said to date from an incident at Harvard University in 1945.

There was a problem with a very early mainframe computer when a moth became trapped in the circuits. From then on, when anything went wrong with it the programmers would blame the *bugs*.

While this story is undoubtedly true, the reality is that the first recorded use of the word in this context is in the following quote from the *Pall Mall Gazette* of 11 March 1889:

"Mr. Edison, I was informed, had been up the two previous nights discovering 'a bug' in his phonograph - an expression for solving a difficulty, and implying that some imaginary insect has secreted itself inside and is causing all the trouble."

note

Unit testing and integration testing

You'll often hear the above terminology used in the context of application testing.

Unit testing means the testing that you did as you developed each part of the application (such as testing that you had calculated the correct dates for public holidays).

Integration testing means the testing of the entire application after each of its parts have been assembled into one coherent application.

Integration testing is the phase that you are about to enter after this lesson.

Year Planner-44

Lesson 7-4: Remove test data and finalize the year planner

The year planner is now complete. All that remains is to remove the test data that you entered during development. The application will then be ready to distribute to your users.

1 Open *Year Planner-44* (if it isn't already open).

2 Select the *Custom Events* worksheet if it isn't already selected.

3 Replace all non-recurring custom events with a single event called: **Example Non-Recurring Event**

Removing all events from the tables could make it difficult for a user to understand, so it's best to leave a single example.

1. Right-click on one of the rows in the *Non-recurring* table.

2. Click: Delete→Table Rows from the shortcut menu.

3. Right-click in the table again and delete another row, so that only one row remains.

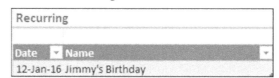

4. In cell A6, type: **01-Jan-2017**

5. In cell B6, type: **Example Non-Recurring Event**

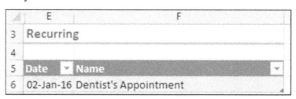

4 Replace all recurring custom events with a single event called: **Example Recurring Event**

1. In the same way as you did before, remove all but one row from the *Recurring* table.

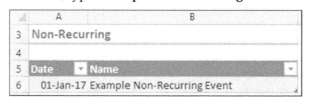

2. In cell E6, type: **02-Jan-2017**

3. In cell F6, type: **Example Recurring Event**

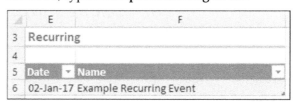

note

The "expert beta tester" problem

When an application is finished but untested, or partially tested, it is usually called a *beta version*.

It is common to make beta test versions available to interested users so that they can report problems before an application is more widely distributed.

Users that express an interest in test-driving the beta versions are usually "expert users" (the most enthusiastic, experienced and technically-aware users in the organisation).

Often an application will suddenly encounter all sorts of problems when released to real users – even though the expert users who did the testing found it to be perfect.

The problem is caused by novice, inexperienced, users doing things in unusual ways. They click in the "wrong" places, do things in a very peculiar sequence, and press odd keystroke combinations.

Because the "expert users" do everything in a clean and logical way, many errors are not discovered.

For this reason, the very best testers are not the "expert users" but the most inexperienced and computer-phobic users.

Your application needs to be reliable, bullet-proof and error-free for all users irrespective of how they choose to use it.

5   Select the *Calendar* worksheet.

6   Use the calendar controls to display January 2017.

7   Save the workbook as *Year Planner-Final*.

The year planner is now complete and ready for use.

8   Confirm that your application satisfies all the requirements detailed in the functional specification.

When an application is complete you should work through the functional specification ticking off each feature to confirm that it works as specified.

9   Complete integration testing.

Because you have only just finished your application it is likely that some parts of it might not function exactly as planned (software developers refer to these teething issues as *bugs*).

If there are any obvious bugs it is better that you find and repair them before releasing the application to your users.

You may wish to create a test document in which you record your testing along with screen grabs.

10   Distribute your beta application to a limited number of users.

A newly developed application that has not yet benefited from the test of time is often referred to as a *beta version*.

You should begin by distributing your beta application to a selected group of beta testers (see sidebar). They can report any issues back to you and you can then fix any bugs found and then release a new version.

Your application will gradually become more and more robust until you can declare the version ready for release and make it available to a wider audience.

If a bug is reported, try to replicate it in the *Year Planner Final* workbook in your sample files set. If you are unable to replicate it you will know that there is an error somewhere in your own implementation.

11   Let us know if you think you have found a bug.

You can always download the latest version of the sample file set from the thesmartmethod.com web site. If you find a bug that can be replicated in the latest version of the *Year Planner Final* workbook. please report it to us using the contact form at:

https://thesmartmethod.com/contact/

This book is regularly updated to support new versions of Excel. The year planner will always have "no known bugs" when each update is released.

Appendix A: Skills Covered in the Essential Skills Course

Construction kits are of most value to competent Excel users who have already mastered all of the skills used in the kit but need to get better at applying them to real-world projects.

It is possible to attempt to use this book to learn Excel "by rote" – following the instructions for each step without really understanding what you are doing. While many readers will find this enjoyable, it isn't sufficient (on its own) to fully master Excel.

Excel is a huge and daunting application and is packed with useful functionality that you can effectively learn with our two tutorials (*Essential Skills* and *Expert Skills*).

If you now progress to our *Essential Skills* course, you'll have an in-depth appreciation of many of the skills you have used in this construction kit. You'll also learn a vast number of skills and techniques that were not needed to complete this construction kit.

If you train to *Essential Skills* level, you will have Excel skills that would impress any employer. Your Excel skills will be better than most office workers (even those with many years of Excel experience).

This appendix lists all the lessons contained in the eight sessions that make up the latest version of the *Essential Skills* book (our books are updated at least once every six months). There are also video walk-throughs (provided on the thesmartmethod.com web site) for each lesson in the book.

Learn *Excel 2019 Essential Skills with The Smart Method* is available as both a low-cost printed paper book (always in stock at Amazon) and as an unlocked, printable, PDF e-Book available for instant download from the https://thesmartmethod.com web site.

Essential skills course outline

Session 1: Basic Skills

▓ Start Excel and open a new blank workbook

▓ Check that your Excel version is up to date

▓ Change the Office Theme

▓ Maximize, minimize, re-size, move and close the Excel window

▓ Download the sample files and open/navigate a workbook

▓ Save a workbook to a local file

▓ Understand common file formats

▓ Pin a workbook and understand file organization

▓ View, move, add, rename, delete and navigate worksheet tabs

▓ Use the Versions feature to recover an unsaved Draft file

▓ Use the Versions feature to recover an earlier version of a workbook

▓ Use the Ribbon

▓ Understand Ribbon components

▓ Customize the Quick Access Toolbar and preview the printout

▓ Use the Mini Toolbar, Key Tips and keyboard shortcuts

▓ Understand views

▓ Hide and show the Formula Bar and Ribbon

▓ Use the Tell Me help system

▓ Use other help features

Session 2: Doing Useful Work with Excel

▓ Enter text and numbers into a worksheet

▓ Create a new workbook and view two workbooks at the same time

▓ Use AutoSum to quickly calculate totals

▓ Select a range of cells and understand Smart Tags

▓ Enter data into a range and copy data across a range

▓ Select adjacent and non-adjacent rows and columns

▓ Select non-contiguous cell ranges and view summary information

▓ AutoSelect a range of cells

▓ Re-size rows and columns

▓ Use AutoSum to sum a non-contiguous range

▓ Use AutoSum to quickly calculate average and maximum values

- Create your own formulas
- Create functions using Formula AutoComplete
- Use AutoFill for text and numeric series
- Use AutoFill to adjust formulas
- Use AutoFill Options
- Speed up your AutoFills and create a custom fill series
- Understand linear and exponential series
- Use Flash Fill to split and concatenate text
- Use the zoom control
- Print out a worksheet

Session 3: Taking Your Skills to the Next Level

- Insert and delete rows and columns
- Use AutoComplete and fill data from adjacent cells
- Cut, copy and paste
- Cut, copy and paste using drag and drop
- Use Paste Values
- Increase/decrease decimal places displayed
- Transpose a range
- Use the Multiple Item Clipboard
- Use Undo and Redo
- Insert, View and Print cell comments
- Understand absolute, relative and mixed cell references
- Understand templates and set the default custom template folder
- Create a template
- Use a template
- Add an Office Add-In to a workbook
- Freeze columns and rows
- Split the window into multiple panes
- Check spelling

Session 4: Making Your Worksheets Look Professional

- Format dates
- Understand date serial numbers
- Format numbers using built-in number formats

- Create custom number formats

- Horizontally and Vertically align the contents of cells

- Merge cells, wrap text and expand/collapse the formula bar

- Understand themes

- Use cell styles and change themes

- Add color and gradient effects to cells

- Add borders and lines

- Create your own custom theme

- Create your own custom cell styles

- Use a master style book to merge styles

- Use simple conditional formatting

- Manage multiple conditional formats using the Rules Manager

- Bring data alive with visualizations

- Create a formula driven conditional format

- Insert a Sparkline into a range of cells

- Apply a common vertical axis and formatting to a Sparkline group

- Apply a date axis to a Sparkline group and format a single Sparkline

- Use the Format Painter

- Rotate text

Session 5: Charts and Graphics

- Understand chart types, layouts and styles

- Create a simple chart with two clicks

- Move, re-size, copy and delete a chart

- Create a chart using the Recommended Charts feature

- Add and remove chart elements using Quick Layout

- Apply a pre-defined chart style and color set

- Manually format a chart element

- Format 3-D elements and add drop shadows

- Move, re-size, add, position and delete chart elements

- Apply a chart filter

- Change a chart's source data

- Assign non-contiguous source data to a chart

- Understand Data Series and Categories

- Change source data using the Select Data Source dialog tools

- Chart non-contiguous source data by hiding rows and columns

- Create a chart with numerical axes
- Deal with empty data points
- Add data labels to a chart
- Add data labels from a range
- Highlight specific data points with color and annotations
- Add gridlines and scale axes
- Emphasize data by manipulating pie charts
- Create a chart with two vertical axes
- Create a combination chart containing different chart types
- Work with trend lines and forecast sheets
- Add a gradient fill to a chart background
- Create your own chart templates
- Create a filled map chart

Session 6: Working with Multiple Worksheets and Workbooks

- View the same workbook in different windows
- View two windows side by side and perform synchronous scrolling
- Duplicate worksheets within a workbook
- Move and copy worksheets from one workbook to another
- Hide and unhide a worksheet
- Create cross worksheet formulas
- Understand worksheet groups
- Use find and replace

Session 7: Printing Your Work

- Print Preview and change paper orientation
- Use Page Layout view to adjust margins
- Use Page Setup to set margins more precisely and center the worksheet
- Set paper size and scale
- Insert, delete and preview page breaks
- Adjust page breaks using Page Break Preview
- Add auto-headers and auto-footers and set the starting page number
- Add custom headers and footers
- Specify different headers and footers for the first, odd and even pages
- Print only part of a worksheet

- Add row and column data labels and grid lines to printed output

- Print several selected worksheets and change the page order

- Suppress error messages in printouts

Session 8: Cloud Computing

- Understand Cloud Computing

- Save a workbook to a OneDrive

- Open a workbook from a OneDrive

- Understand operating systems and devices

- Understand Office versions

- Understand Excel Online

- Open a workbook using Excel Online

- Share a link to a workbook

- Understand OneDrive AutoSave and Version History

- Edit a workbook simultaneously with other users using Excel Online

Appendix B: Skills Covered in the follow-on Expert Skills Course

Not many Excel users will need to go further than *Essential Skills* in expanding their skill set. Some users may have special requirements, or simply a desire to understand **absolutely every** Excel feature. For such users, we created our *Expert Skills* book that builds upon the skills learned in the *Essential Skills* book.

The *Expert Skills* book teaches advanced Excel skills that are rarely mastered by Excel users.

By the end of the book you'll be a true Excel expert. Your Excel skills will be greater and broader than almost all other Excel users in the workplace.

This appendix lists all of the lessons contained in the eleven sessions that make up the *Expert Skills* book.

Learn *Excel 2019 Expert Skills with The Smart Method* is available as both a low-cost printed paper book (always in stock at Amazon) and as an e-Book, provided in unlocked, printable PDF format (as are all of our e-books).

You can only obtain the *Expert Skills* e-Book from the https://thesmartmethod.com web site (this is the publisher's own web site: The Smart Method Ltd).

Expert skills course outline

Session 1: Tables, and Ranges

- Understand update channels
- Check that automatic updates are enabled
- Change the Office Theme
- Apply a simple filter to a range
- Apply a top 10 and custom filter to a range
- Apply an advanced filter with multiple OR criteria
- Apply an advanced filter with complex criteria
- Apply an advanced filter with function-driven criteria
- Extract unique records using an advanced filter
- Add totals using Quick Analysis
- Add percentage and running totals using Quick Analysis
- Convert a range into a table and add a total row
- Format a table using table styles and convert a table into a range
- Create a custom table style
- Sort a range or table by rows
- Sort a range by columns
- Sort a range or table by custom list
- Name a table and create an automatic structured table reference
- Create a manual structured table reference
- Use special items in structured table references
- Understand unqualified structured table references

Session 2: Data Integrity, Subtotals and Validations

- Split fixed width data using Text to Columns
- Split delimited data using Text to Columns
- Automatically subtotal a range
- Create nested subtotals
- Consolidate data from multiple data ranges
- Use data consolidation to generate quick subtotals from tables
- Validate numerical data
- Create user-friendly messages for validation errors
- Create data validation input messages

- Add a formula-driven date validation and a text length validation
- Add a table-based dynamic list validation
- Use a formula-driven custom validation to enforce complex business rules
- Remove duplicate values from a table
- Use a custom validation to add a unique constraint to a column

Session 3: Advanced Functions

- Understand precedence rules and use the Evaluate feature
- Use common functions with Formula AutoComplete
- Use the Insert Function dialog and the PMT function
- Use the PV and FV functions to value investments
- Use the IF logic function
- Use the SUMIF and COUNTIF functions to create conditional totals
- Understand date serial numbers
- Understand common date functions
- Use the DATEDIF function
- Use date offsets to manage projects using the scheduling equation
- Use the DATE function to offset days, months and years
- Enter time values and perform basic time calculations
- Perform time calculations that span midnight
- Understand common time functions and convert date serial numbers to decimal values
- Use the TIME function to offset hours, minutes and seconds
- Use the AND and OR functions to construct complex Boolean criteria
- Understand calculation options (manual and automatic)
- Concatenate strings using the concatenation operator (&)
- Use the TEXT function to format numerical values as strings
- Extract text from fixed width strings using the LEFT, RIGHT and MID functions
- Extract text from delimited strings using the FIND and LEN functions
- Use a VLOOKUP function for an exact or inexact lookup
- Use an IFERROR function to suppress error messages
- Use the SWITCH, MATCH, INDEX and IFS functions

Session 4: Using Names and the Formula Auditing Tools

- Automatically create single-cell range names
- Manually create single cell range names and named constants
- Use range names to make formulas more readable
- Automatically create range names in two dimensions

- Use intersection range names and the INDIRECT function
- Create dynamic formula-based range names using the OFFSET function
- Create table based dynamic range names
- Create two linked drop-down lists using range names
- Understand the #NUM!, #DIV/0! and #NAME? error values
- Understand the #VALUE!, #REF! and #NULL! error values
- Understand background error checking and error checking rules
- Manually check a worksheet for errors
- Audit a formula by tracing precedents
- Audit a formula by tracing dependents
- Use the Watch Window to monitor cell values
- Use Speak Cells to eliminate data entry errors

Session 5: What If Analysis and Security

- Create a single-input data table
- Create a two-input data table
- Define scenarios
- Create a scenario summary report
- Use Goal Seek
- Use Solver
- Hide and unhide worksheets, columns and rows
- Create custom views
- Prevent unauthorized users from opening or modifying workbooks
- Control the changes users can make to workbooks
- Restrict the cells users are allowed to change
- Allow different levels of access to a worksheet with multiple passwords
- Create a digital certificate
- Add an invisible digital signature to a workbook
- Add a visible digital signature to a workbook

Session 6: Working with Hyperlinks, Other Applications and Workgroups

- Hyperlink to worksheets and ranges
- Hyperlink to other workbooks and the Internet
- Hyperlink to an e-mail address and enhance the browsing experience
- Embed an Excel worksheet object into a Word document

- Embed an Excel chart object into a Word document

- Link an Excel worksheet to a Word document

- Understand the three different ways to share a workbook

- Share a workbook using the lock method

- Share a workbook using the merge method

- Share a workbook on a network

- Accept and reject changes to shared workbooks

Session 7: Forms and Macros

- Add group box and option button controls to a worksheet form

- Add a combo box control to a worksheet form

- Set form control cell links

- Connect result cells to a form

- Add a check box control to a worksheet form

- Use check box data in result cells

- Add a temperature gauge chart to a form

- Add a single input data table to a form

- Improve form appearance and usability

- Understand macros and VBA

- Record a macro with absolute references

- Understand macro security

- Implement macro security

- Understand trusted documents

- Record a macro with relative references

- Use shapes to run macros

- Run a macro from a button control

- Show and hide Ribbon tabs

- Add custom groups to standard Ribbon tabs

- Create a custom Ribbon tab

Session 8: Pivot Tables

- Create a one-dimensional pivot table report from a table

- Create a grouped pivot table report

- Understand pivot table rows and columns

- Understand the pivot table data cache

- Apply a simple filter and sort to a pivot table
- Use report filter fields
- Filter a pivot table visually using slicers
- Add a timeline control to a pivot table
- Use slicers to create a custom timeline
- Use report filter fields to automatically create multiple pages
- Format a pivot table using PivotTable styles
- Create a custom pivot table style
- Understand pivot table report layouts
- Add/remove subtotals and apply cell styles to pivot table fields
- Display multiple summations within a single pivot table
- Add a calculated field to a pivot table
- Add a calculated item to a pivot table
- Group by text, date and numeric value ranges
- Show row data by percentage of total rather than value
- Use pivot table values in simple formulas
- Use the GETPIVOTDATA function
- Create a pivot chart from a pivot table
- Embed multiple pivot tables onto a worksheet
- Use slicers to filter multiple pivot tables

Sessions 9-11 cover OLAP technology

Microsoft introduced some extremely sophisticated OLAP (On Line Analytical Processing) tools into Excel 2013. This was further expanded in Excel 2019. OLAP skills are not commonly found in Excel users (even IT professionals often struggle with data modeling and OLAP concepts).

Recognizing that OLAP skills will not be needed by many users (even Excel experts) we placed the OLAP related skills into the last three sessions of the Expert skills book.

These sessions cover not only the new OLAP related features, but also the relational modeling theory needed to understand and use them. Full coverage is given to the new OLAP pivot table (a new type of pivot table that can be used with an OLAP data source).

OLAP is the key to working with Big Data (in an Excel context, Big Data is data that has more than a million rows). In the OLAP sessions you'll sometimes work with very large data sets that contain well over a million rows (exceeding the capacity of an Excel worksheet).

Session 9: Data Modeling, OLAP and Business Intelligence

- Import tables from an external relational database
- Understand primary and foreign keys
- Link primary and foreign keys using VLOOKUP

- Efficiently import data using a view
- Understand linked tables
- Work with big data
- Create a simple data model
- Understand OLAP pivot tables
- Understand OLAP cubes and Business Intelligence
- Create an OLAP pivot table directly from a relational database
- Understand many-to-many relationships
- Create an OLAP pivot table using a many-to-many relationship
- Understand MDX queries and OLAP pivot table limitations
- Use the CUBEVALUE function to query an OLAP cube
- Convert CUBEVALUE functions to include MDX expressions
- Create an asymmetric OLAP pivot table using Named Sets

Session 10: 3D Maps

- Create a simple 3D Map
- Confirm the accuracy of geocoding
- Map using different location fields
- Apply filters to a 3D Map
- Set layer options and customize data cards
- Add a height field to a layer
- Apply different visualization types
- Visualize multiple categories
- Create a visualization with multiple layers
- Add annotations
- Create a video from temporal data
- Set scene options
- Create a tour with multiple scenes

Session 11: Create Get & Transform queries

- Understand Get & Transform and ETL
- Create a simple extract and load web query
- Understand queries and connections
- Move, remove, rename, filter and sort columns
- Split delimited data

- Specify data types

- Understand steps and PQFL

- Remove empty, error and top and bottom rows

- Understand and work with null values

- Transform date and time columns

- Transform number columns

- Add a custom calculated column

- Create an aggregated data query

- Unpivot aggregated data

- Work with multiple queries

- Create an append query

- Understand normal and de-normalized data

- Create a simple two-table merged query

- Create a five-table merged query

- Edit a workbook simultaneously with other users using Excel Online

Index

Moving to the next level

Essential Skills teaches Excel from first principles

The *Essential Skills* book is published in both Excel 2019 and Excel 365 editions. By the end of the book you will have excellent Excel skills, good enough to impress any employer.

The paper printed book is always in stock at Amazon.

The e-book is published in unlocked, printable PDF format (all of our e-books are published in this way) and is only available from https://thesmartmethod.com (this is the publisher's own web site).

The next book in the series (Expert Skills) covers only the most advanced Excel features

The *Expert Skills* book is published in both Excel 2019 and Excel 365 editions. This book will give you advanced Excel skills that are rarely mastered by the average user. By the end of the book you'll be a true Excel expert, able to use all of the power available from the world's most powerful business tool. Your Excel skills will be greater and broader than almost all other Excel users in the workplace.

The paper printed book is always in stock at Amazon.

The e-book is published in unlocked, printable PDF format (all of our e-books are published in this way) and is only available from https://thesmartmethod.com (this is the publisher's own web site).

Excel Challenges

Our Excel online challenges are a little like the exercises at the end of each session in this book. Unlike the exercises, the online challenges will test the application of many skills (covered in different sessions in the book).

We began trialling challenges in July 2018 and (at time of writing in November 2018) we'd published three challenges but by the time you read this book we may have produced more.

Access the challenges online at:

https://thesmartmethod.com/excel-challenges/

Use your new Excel skills to teach your own classroom courses

If you work through our *Essential Skills* and *Expert Skills* books carefully you will become a true Excel expert. There is a huge demand, everywhere in the world, for Excel training at all levels. The skills you have learned in the books will enable you to teach both introductory Excel courses (providing all of the skills needed by most office workers) and expert-level Excel courses.

Our books are available for all Excel versions in common use (Excel 2007, 2010, 2013, 2016, 2019 and 365 for Windows along with Excel 2016 & 2019 for Apple Mac). You can use the books as courseware during your classes and then give each student a copy of the book to take home as reference material when the course is over.

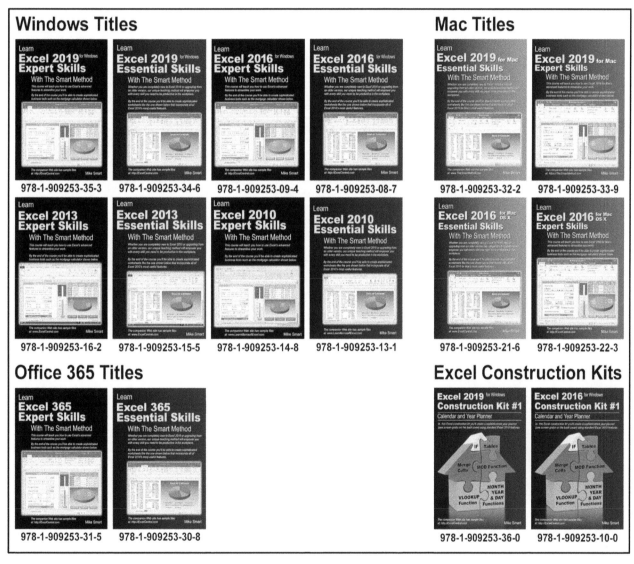

You can quote the ISBN numbers shown above to any book retailer or wholesaler. All major distributors (in every country of the world) have our books in stock for immediate delivery.

Place a direct order for 5+ books for wholesale prices and free delivery worldwide

To place a publisher-direct order you only need to order five books or more (of the same title). To view wholesale prices, go to this web page: https://thesmartmethod.com/wholesale-printed-books